More Small Trimarans

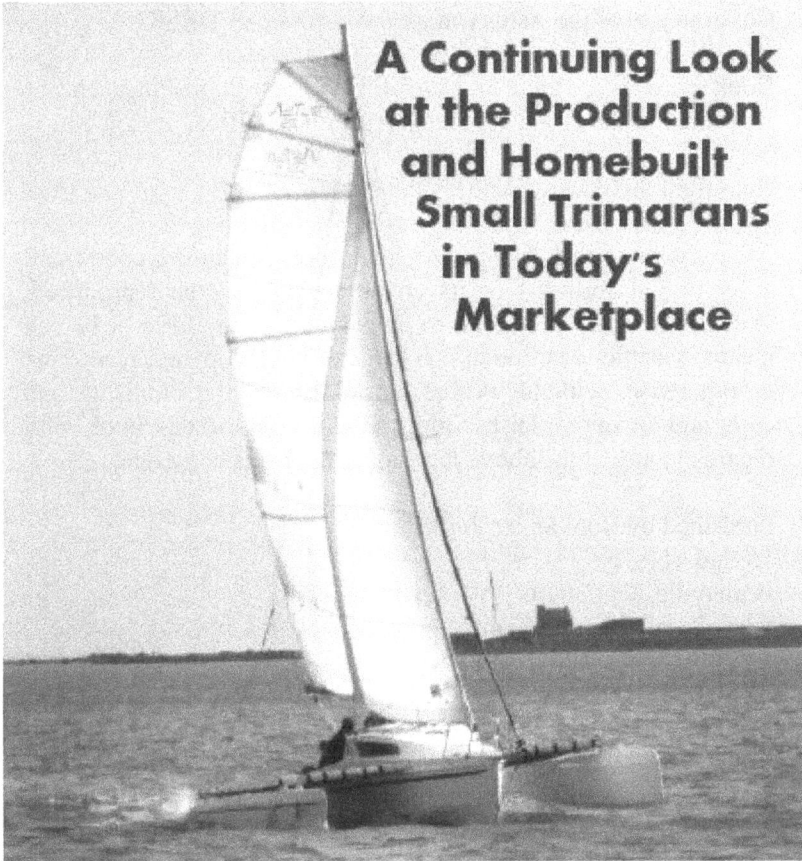

A Continuing Look at the Production and Homebuilt Small Trimarans in Today's Marketplace

www.SmallTrimarans.com

Joe Farinaccio

BookSpecs Publishing
Pennsville, NJ

More Small Trimarans

Published by BookSpecs Publishing
16 Sunset Ave.
Pennsville, NJ 08070
www.SmallTrimarans.com

ISBN 978-0-9721461-3-5
LCCN 2010900205

This book is available as a product for both affiliate selling and also as a product for special joint ventures with entrepreneurs, booksellers and/or blog owners in the sailing and marine industry. Visit www.SmallTrimarans.com and contact the author for more information about how you can make money with it.

Legal Notice

The publisher and author have attempted to verify the accuracy of the information contained in this publication. But neither party assumes any responsibilities for errors, omissions or contradictory information contained therein. The publisher and author are not liable or responsible for any losses or damages, which include, but aren't limited to: loss of personal assets (tangible or intangible), information, service, profits, business, clients or other pecuniary loss. The information contained within this publication is not intended as advice – personal, consumer, financial, legal, medical, or otherwise. This publication's information is being provided for educational purposes only. The reader is encouraged to seek the advice of a professional whenever applicable. The owner or reader of this publication assumes full and complete responsibility for the use of this material and all related information. Joe Farinaccio, BookSpecs Publishing and SmallTrimarans.com do not assume any responsibility or liability with regards to these materials on behalf of the reader whatsoever.

Additional Notice and Disclaimers

Any results stated or implied within this publication should be considered atypical, and not guaranteed results. No promises, suggestions or guarantees are made in this publication, whether stated or implied. Results may vary from one individual to another from anything that has been stated or implied. All information, including resources found within, are not to be taken as endorsements. This publication may contain advice, strategies or suggestions that are not suitable for your situation. All information is being provided on an "at your own risk" basis.

While the publisher and author have done their best to make sure this publication is enjoyable, certain typographical or grammatical errors may exist. Any errors, including any that may be perceived as slight of a specific group, individual, person or organization, are completely unintentional. Whenever the neuter isn't used then it means any one gender was chosen for the sake of simplicity. This publication was created with the goal that its contents might be found useful to readers. It should not be scrutinized for other purposes, including writing style, language correctness or gender equality.

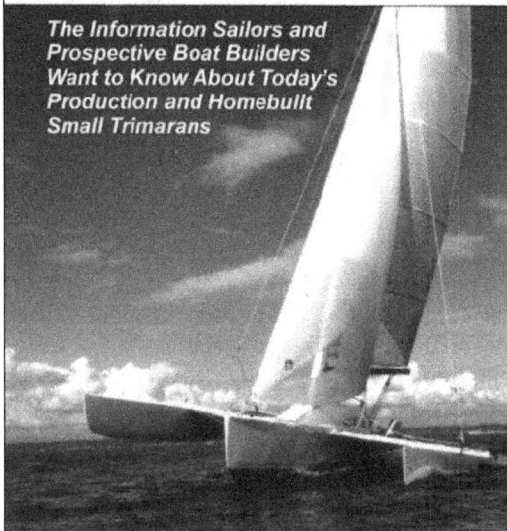

**This book is dedicated
to my brother,**

Paul Francis Farinaccio (*Paulie*)

Contents

Introduction

At the beginning of *Small Trimarans: An Introduction*, I wrote, *"I've completed many writing projects in my time, but I don't ever remember having as much fun as I had with this one."* And how true it was.

So what new writing project could possibly come close? One that results in *another* book about small trimarans, of course! Except this time, I tried to make it even *better*.

This second book includes more interviews and more pictures than the first one. In addition, I really made an effort to contact some notable designers who live outside of the United States, including those from Canada, France, New Zealand, Australia and the United Kingdom.

The format for this book is essentially the same. I sought out the assumed experts (mostly accomplished boat designers) and spoke with each one about the small trimaran(s) they'd conceived of – and often built themselves in most cases. They are passionate multihull enthusiasts. And although I realize that "passion" isn't a substitute for creating a truly excellent boat design, I appreciate it regardless. At least those featured in this book were willing to put in the time and effort to create something and then believe in it enough to offer it in the marketplace.

This book takes up where the other one left off, which is trying to find out more about other small trimaran designs out there in the world today. What this means is that while I wasn't able to talk about *every* small tri out there, I've probably covered *most* of the boats available at this time between the first book and this second one.

All in all, there is plenty of reading material in these pages to keep enthusiastic readers busy ... and coming back periodically to digest more information, as favorite sections are re-read. It's not only fun reading about each boat, it's also enjoyable to learn the stories *behind* them, which includes a brief background about most of the designers interviewed.

Fact Versus Fiction

This book, like the first volume, isn't filled with *technical* details. One person who read the first book chastised me over this, saying that if there wasn't "hard data" available to back up each and every claim made by somebody about their boat then any such claims were "nonsense." (Actually, this sailor used another noun ... but you get the idea).

To be honest, I think the man had a totally valid point. *In the end, there is no substitute for pure facts grounded in reality.* But I also think this reader missed the basic purpose of the book. The goal wasn't to create a *Small Trimaran Encyclopedia*. The aim was to record conversations with designers that included a little about where they came from, how they got into sailing, and then progress into the story behind the development of their featured boat(s).

The "hard facts," meaning technical data, can (and should) be obtained directly from designers themselves. They should also be willing to offer potential customers contact information for 3rd parties who can verify undocumented claims. And I strongly urge potential customers and/or boat builders who are considering buying a boat or plans to get all of their questions answered *before* handing over hard-earned money to anyone.

I'm certain the small trimaran designers featured in this book are all biased in favor of their designs. That is to be expected.

Introduction

And it's certainly possible that a few guys may have embellished a fact or two. (*I hope not ... but it's certainly possible*)!

That being said, where does one begin learning about such boats and doing background research? Or how can a small tri lover simply get in some good "armchair sailing"? I think having a good conversation with multihull devotees who've designed the very boats that capture our attention is a great way to *begin*.

Small tri fans want to know more about these fascinating watercraft. And since this book covers production (or commercially produced) boats and homebuilt models, there are lots of features and styles to consider. It's inevitable that each reader will be attracted to different trimarans for various reasons. Although most of us are probably in agreement with legendary trimaran designer Dick Newick, who wrote, "*People sail for fun and no one has yet convinced me that it's more fun to go slow than it is to go fast.*"

A Final Word About The Featured Designers

Most of the guys I interviewed reviewed their chapter for the book in order to make sure that I'd transcribed their information correctly. Ed Horstman didn't participate in a full interview, but he did allow me to ask him a few questions, then he asked me to use the wording (verbatim at some points) from written material that he wrote and published himself a while back, in order to write the *TriStar 18* chapter in 3rd person.

As you will see, when it came to speaking to a couple of my French participants, the language barrier was so tough that I had to submit written questions to them. Then they received help from others who spoke English a little better than they did in order to try and cull together some interesting material for readers about their boat. These situations are noted and such sections are easily recognizable in the book.

More Small Trimarans

I'd hoped to include interviews with the developers of the Corsair and TelStar trimarans. After initially meeting these gentlemen at the big boat show in Annapolis, MD they seemed willing to participate in this project. But in the end, the publishing deadline ended without me being able to conduct interviews with them.

It's important to note that while most of the questions asked of each interviewee were "similar," they weren't always the "same." None of these gentlemen, however, ever knew what questions were asked of someone else. Nor did they ever know what contrary opinions (if any) were expressed by anyone else I interviewed.

As the reader, keep in mind that these boat designers *do* express differing opinions occasionally. One designer's opinion, however, was never purposely pitted against another's. The opinions shared in this book were simply attempts to answer specific questions posed within a certain context. This means that you, as the reader, must dig further if you want to clarify any concept being talked about within these pages.

In closing, I'd like to thank a few members of the small trimaran community who volunteered to be proofreaders after I put out a call for help: Jim Kearns, Cord Runne, Donnally King, Barney Gulley and Mark & Cheryl Ruesink. And I'd like to once again thank the designers who are featured in this book for participating in this project. And I need to thank you, the reader, for supporting this work by obtaining a copy of this book. I hope you enjoy reading about these small trimarans as much as I enjoyed transcribing and publishing this material.

-- *Small Tri Guy*

Chapter 1

An Interview with Mark Zollitsch

Designer of the Adventure Trimaran

I grew up on the coast of Maine. An enthusiastic sailor, boater and professor, my father had most summers off to take us sailing in one of the best water playgrounds in the world! So my years growing up as a boy included significant amounts of sailing, kayaking and canoeing.

Back around 1975 Dad bought a Venture 22 pop-top trailer-sailer. Sometimes the whole family would go out in it and sometimes just my father and I would go. We'd sometimes go out camp-cruising for weeks at a time, exploring the prolific islands, bays and peninsulas of the Maine coastline.

These were wonderful experiences growing up; they really established my love for the water, wind, waves and all the sights and smells of the ocean. Sailing isn't just a mechanical experience; it's something that allows for all of your senses to be engaged.

My idea for the Adventure Trimaran came, in part, from 12 years of being on the U.S. Canoe and Kayak team. That background led to a passion for both paddle-sports and outrigger canoes. I'd been looking for a boat that sort of blended the ability to paddle with an ability to sail it.

I love Farrier-type trimarans. I'm blessed to be able to skipper an F-31 up here in the Pacific Northwest. But a boat like that weighs thousands of pounds and isn't "paddle" material. I was thinking about something that could be both paddled and sailed.

One day, after coming across the Watertribe website (http://www.watertribe.com), I read about the Everglades Challenge and got the idea to design a boat myself that blended the best of both worlds - paddling and sailing. The goal was to produce something light and skinny enough to allow for both. At the time I came up with the Adventure tri design I didn't think anything like it existed. So that's what I set out to do.

When designing this boat, my tendency was to apply a very "hands-on" approach. Professional designers will sit down on a computer first in order to design. Being a do-it-yourself type of person, I just shaped out my model instead.

"Keep Things Simple"

Aside from referring to some sketches that I'd made, I simply drew upon what I knew about both sailing hulls and the shapes of paddle-craft. I took huge chunks of foam and started making a form, shaping it as I went along with a beaver saw and a cheese-grater type sure-form. That proved to be a lot of work, of course, especially getting all of the lines fair and true. But I really enjoyed that part of the process.

An Interview with Mark Zollitsch

The original hull shapes were formed using foam; the final prototype sailboat was made with a foam core laminate. I have a local friend named Sterling who specializes in using these materials. He is a "wonder worker," and runs *Sterling's Kayaks and Fiberglass* in Bellingham, WA. He is an expert with resin infusion and was able to take the molds I'd made and create a super-light carbon fiber foam core laminate, which was then resin-infused. This is a great process because you not only save weight, but the resin is infused evenly throughout the core and there are no dry spots or wasted resin.

More Small Trimarans

I studied the challenge of how to connect the akas with the main hull in depth. When you have boats that are beach cat size there are certain challenges and obstacles. I looked at the possibility of using some type of sliding system or folding system for the outriggers. But when you look at a folding mechanism, especially ones used on bigger boats like Farriers, then you're obviously dealing with larger craft where it makes more sense using it.

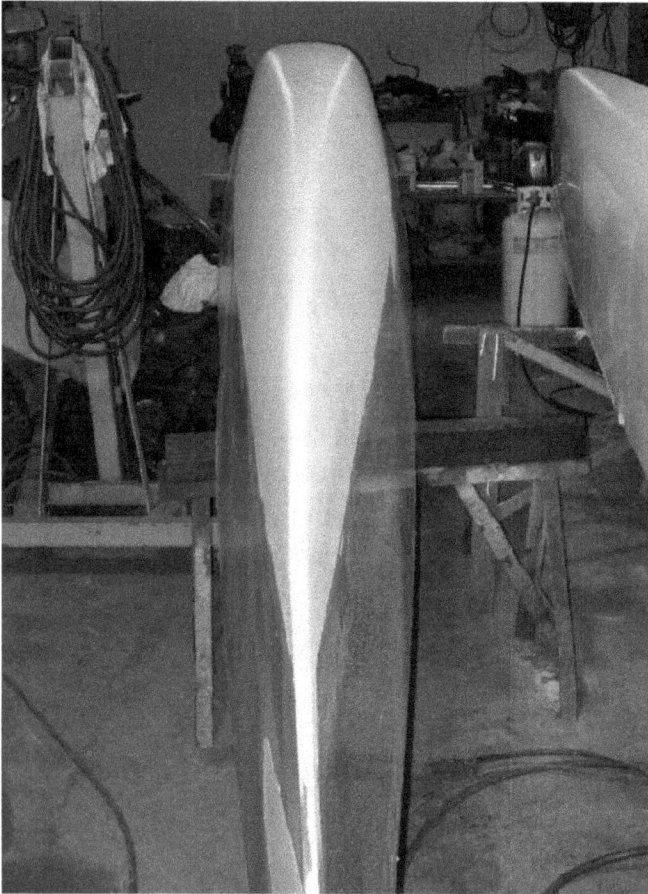

Folding systems add weight, complexity and expense. There are diminishing returns when it comes to using a folding system on smaller boats. So I finally decided to keep things simple and just use carbon tubes that are held in place by caps that bolt into the hulls.

Since building the Adventure Trimaran, the Weta company came out with a system that I like very much too. They developed a great way of attaching the amas to their main hull with a "sliding socket" system.

The issue of how to attach nets is also a question that comes up when building a small trimaran. There are different ways of attaching nets to crossbeams. But I know from experience that the more you can attach hard pieces to hard pieces the easier the process is going to be. It also allows for a boat's setup at the sailing venue to go faster.

Creating sleeves on the nets that allow crossbeams to simply slide into them is a good solution, if you can make it work, because using lacing to attach the nets to beams takes lots of time. The more you can avoid lacing the better off you're going to be. Using zippers can also make things go faster and is generally more convenient too.

I attached the trampolines using sleeves and spring-loaded tie downs on my Adventure Trimaran prototype ... similar to what you see on car-top roof racks. There are straps, which are cinched down and secure the trampolines without too much trouble.

The actual trampoline material I first used is readily available to homebuilders and one of the least expensive items they're going to need to purchase when building a sailboat like this. There are abundant sources of this material for the nets. The builder just needs to get the webbing stitched to meet his or her size requirements. Most of the time, you can simply use the same kind of netting material found on outdoor trampolines.

The black-colored material commonly used on outdoor trampolines today isn't springy. It's the actual springs on outdoor trampolines that make the material appear to be springy in itself. This tramp material is very strong and UV resistant since it's made to be outside all the time. This makes it a good choice for trampoline material on small tris.

Some other netting materials out there are actually lighter and stronger than the outdoor trampoline material, although they're a bit more expensive. Some allow the wind and water to blow easily through the netting in both directions.

"Fast Going Downwind"

The Adventure Trimaran's main hull is set up with seats in the middle of it that have footwells. The sailor can be seated in a comfortable position in order to paddle the boat (if he or she has to). This is a huge difference from almost any other sailboat, except for something like a Raptor 16, which is also designed to be a good single person sail-paddle type of watercraft, which I have also enjoyed sailing.

I've done a good bit of paddling and sailing in the Adventure tri. If there is low wind then you can simultaneously sail and paddle in order to significantly increase the apparent wind and hence the boat's speed. When the wind comes back up then you can go quite fast by shifting your weight on the boat to counter the heeling force, just as on other small trimarans.

The open, light design of this trimaran led me to choose a schooner rig for it. When you get into putting a 30 to 35-foot mast on a boat, like you see on fast beach cats such as a Tornado or Nacra 6.0, then you're getting to the point where one person can't easily handle the amount of sail area by himself or herself.

More Small Trimarans

This is especially true if they're out on the water in the middle of the night sailing during an event like the Everglades Challenge. The schooner rig configuration I chose for this boat broke things down so the boat just doesn't have lots of heeling force. It's much more manageable in higher winds for a single individual.

The schooner rig setup turned out to be a good way to get more sail area onto this boat without having to put a single rig high into the air. The schooner rig, of course, isn't as efficient for tacking upwind. When you're tacking upwind then the front sail partially blankets the rear sail and there is some airfoil interference going on and it's not as efficient as the single rig. This slows things down a bit when going upwind, but not excessively so.

Every design is a trade-off though and this boat was meant to be manageable given the circumstances. You don't see a schooner rig on many multihulls out there but it works well with this boat. When you crack off a bit, and you're reaching or running, then it's fabulous because you get the advantage of all that sail area. This boat is particularly fast going downwind. It can hit 20 knots on a reach.

The masts I chose for the schooner rig on this particular boat was driven by a desire to use material that is simple, easy to use, and relatively inexpensive to either repair or replace if something breaks. The solution was really obvious to me -- windsurfer masts. They're widely available and not super expensive.

Windsurfing masts aren't what you might call "super-cheap," but they're about half the price of a similar-sized custom fabricated carbon spar and readily available. Manufacturers crank out windsurfer masts on an assembly line. Some windsurfer masts are composed of about 18% and 20% fiberglass to lower cost and increase the shatter resistance of pure carbon.

They worked out great for this trimaran. I put fasteners onto 2 of these masts and glued a track on back to hold the sails in place. Each mast is held in place by an upper and lower stay but no diamond stays -- like maxi-trimarans. The configuration works very well. And virtually all of the controls for both sails are easily accessible from the main seat on the center hull.

The length of time it takes to set this boat up to go sailing depends upon how many times you've done it and whether or not you have help getting things ready. It generally takes anywhere from a ½ hour to 40 minutes. It would obviously take 2 people less time than a single sailor.

Setting up the rigging generally takes the most amount of time when getting the boat set up to go out on the water. There are small lines that can easily get tangled if you're not careful. And since this boat has 2 rigs, you're essentially doubling the number of lines, sheets, outhauls, cunninghams and all of that stuff. This again, is an example of the trade-offs necessary in any design.

"Out In 30-35 Knot Winds"

The Adventure Trimaran is certainly trailerable. It's actually cartoppable, if you've got a full-sized pickup or large SUV. The main hull is 24-feet long. I've got lots of funny pictures with me carrying the boat on top of my Toyota Corolla, but would not recommend it. It takes a good amount of effort to lift the boat up onto a vehicle, so using a trailer is probably the best way to go for most sailors.

The boat is made primarily for one to two people to go sailing. I've had 3 on it and it sailed okay. But the added weight obviously causes the boat to sit lower in the water. The boat is small and light so any added sailors are going to significantly affect its weight displacement, which is true for any smaller craft … although 2 adults and a child would work pretty well.

Sailing the Adventure Trimaran can be both a dry and somewhat wet experience. If you're going through 3-foot waves then you're going to get a little wet. But if the water is pretty calm and you're only moving through 6 to 8 inch waves then it's a fairly dry ride. You'll be drier on the upwind side anytime you hike out on a trampoline.

One big benefit of this small trimaran is its stability factor … which is huge. The schooner rig really allows for a safe ride. I've had the boat out in 30-35 knot winds and there is no need to reef the sails and the boat is in no danger of flipping at all. This is a much different situation than you'd find yourself in if you were sailing a beach cat.

The danger of going into the drink on a beach cat is much higher than you'll ever have to be concerned about if you're sailing the Adventure Trimaran. It's a very safe and stable sailboat. Even though the windsurfing masts are double-stayed, these masts are designed to bend off a bit at the top when you get a puff and relieve the pressure. That feature works well with its application on this design.

Anytime you're in high winds and getting a gust, the top of the masts bend off a little and allows the pressure to be decreased on the heeling force being exerted at that moment. For new sailors, an Adventure tri would offer exceptional ease-of-use and beginner safety. The lower rigs will prevent most inexperienced sailors from getting into trouble.

"A Fast, Versatile Boat"

The ideal sailor for this tri will probably be able to identify with the name I gave this design. It's made for an adventure-oriented person who isn't all about yacht racing performance, but is looking for an adventure racing or adventure camping experience instead. In other words, they enjoy going fast when sailing but aren't into racing against F-31s and that kind of thing.

The Adventure tri turned out to be a swift, versatile boat that can take 1 to 2 people out for either a day of sailing or a combined sailing/camping experience. Even though it doesn't offer a cabin, this boat is able to go out on the open water and also has enough space to bring along camping gear.

This is a sailboat for someone who is looking for something just a little bit different ... and who is okay with "roughing it." It's also a boat that should appeal to a sea kayaker who wants to do a lot less work at times. It's great for island hopping and camping around. It's possible for sailors to camp out on the nets if they want to. You can pull this boat up on the beach after a day of moving around from place to place and set up camp quickly. It's a really fun, alternative type of small boat.

An Interview with Mark Zollitsch

If somebody wants an Adventure Trimaran kit, they'd acquire the unassembled hull halves, crossbeams and foils from me. Then they'd receive instructions on how to acquire the hardware, assemble the rig and put everything together.

Many small trimaran enthusiasts tend to be hobbyists who like doing things themselves. Not everyone wants to buy a finished boat product. So I have a list of resources and suppliers. For example, I have a great relationship with Joe Waters at *Waters Sails* in the Carolinas who makes high quality sails that work well with the small diameter, lightweight masts featured on this boat. He spent a lot of time refining the shape to match the bend characteristics of the mast, which is essential for good sail shape and high performing sails.

At the time of this writing, the Adventure Trimaran is being offered as a kit as well as a finished boat, although this may change. It may continue being offered to homebuilders, or the molds could be sold to an entrepreneur who wants to turn it into a production boat. I posted videos on YouTube.com featuring the Adventure Trimaran, and have been amazed at the views in such a short time, somewhere over 30,000 views at the time of this interview.

I'm currently working on a new project ... a high-performance racing trimaran that I hope will compete with F-boats and the Multi-23. Russell Brown (Jim Brown's son) has actually helped me with some advice and materials for this new boat. I'm calling it the "*Adventure Trimaran 23.*"

The Adventure Tri 23 is going to carry a large sail on a single mast for competitive PHRF buoy racing. I'm not sure if it's going to be for sale or just personal use. But if I do offer it for sale then it'll probably come in a kit.

I've also worked with boat builder and dealer Mike Leneman on this project. Mike is the U.S. dealer for the Multi 23 trimaran. He has helped me acquire various parts and pieces for this project as well, including an ama from his larger L-7 trimaran, which will be the center hull of this boat after some serious modification. I obtained a Nacra 6.0 Express catamaran, (modified by Randy Smythe with significantly more sail area) and a 31-foot carbon fiber mast, which will become the amas and rig for the boat after more modification.

We're really excited about this. Basically, it's going to be a homebuilder's version of the Multi 23 production trimaran. The goal is to create a light, very fast trimaran that can be assembled fairly quickly at a fraction of the cost. But like any good boat project, it's a lot of work!

....

For more about the Adventure Trimaran visit
http://www.adventuretrimaran.com
Contact information for Mark Zollitsch can be found at this website.

Chapter 2

An Interview with Pascal Guignabaudet

U.K. Agent for The Astus Trimarans

I've been sailing for a long time. I grew up in France and had access to a nearby lake. I enjoyed quite a bit of sailing when I was a kid.

After starting to work as an adult I moved to Paris. I didn't get to do much sailing there. But then, later on, I moved to London and it was much better for sailing opportunities.

The first boat I sailed after moving to the U.K. was a 16-foot keelboat. I was very conscious about having a safe boat because I have 4 children and started sailing with them when the youngest was 20 months old. It seemed safe enough but was very heavy. Then I came across a trimaran ... probably at a boat show. The trimaran concept was really attractive to me, especially its stability and other safety factors.

More Small Trimarans

I really liked the Magnum trimarans and was considering a purchase of one of their models. Then I came across the Astus 20.1, which was the first Astus launched by Astusboats. I decided this trimaran was ideal for my needs because it allowed me to have a small cabin. That was a compelling feature because I wanted to go sailing with my children and a cabin would help serve their needs and give them shelter if it got a bit windy or cold.

I contacted the Astusboats company but they didn't have a representative in the U.K. So I began thinking about getting one of their boats and representing their company here in England. After meeting with the managing director of Astusboats everything just sort of fell into place.

The first boat I marketed was the Astus 20.1 and then I also acquired the Astus 16.1 and 14.1 models. We sold a few boats at first and then sales really picked up. What I discovered is that there are quite a few people who had large boats and were getting rid of them because they didn't want to have all of the fees and maintenance costs associated with them. They still wanted to sail though. Many of them discovered the Astus trimarans and were very attracted to these sailboats.

"Very Easy To Use"

Astusboats offers 4 different models for their trimarans: *the Astus 14.1, Astus 16.1, Astus 20.2 and Astus 22*. The Astus 20.2 is a brand new model that replaces the old Astus 20.1, which a lot of sailors here in Europe became familiar with.

The Astus 14.1 is a little different than the rest of the boats. It's actually more of a skiff with stabilizers than a proper trimaran. In other words, it's a dinghy with floats. The floats help the boat stay manageable. A sailor needs to sail this boat flat and not really try and use the floats when they're sailing it.

An Interview with Pascal Guignabaudet

This boat is ideal for those who like sailing on skiffs but don't want to move around as much as they'd have to on a traditional skiff. Traditional skiffs actually require quite a bit of skill in order to sail them successfully. The Astus 14.1 is much more forgiving. But it offers the same kind of acceleration and speed that skiff sailors enjoy.

This boat is ideal for individual sailors and also places like sailing clubs that feature skiffs for their members. It's also great for those who want to move from an ordinary dinghy into something that is going to give them the higher performance of a skiff.

Astus 14.1 is like a stable skiff

Astus 16.1, Astus 20.2 and Astus 22 are really all sailboats from the same family. Their common feature is the sliding telescopic tubes that support their floats. When you want to launch these boats you simply pull the floats out and lock them in with pins. Then you tighten the attached trampolines. You don't need any tools for these exercises either.

Astus 16.1 under sail and on the beach

An Interview with Pascal Guignabaudet

This is a feature that distinguishes the Astus trimarans from the Magnum tris. You can launch the Astus boats with the floats retracted. Then you can push them out *after* you're already on the water. The boat is stable even when its floats are retracted. Some sailors keep their boats on a mooring and leave the floats extended. At other times, you may want to launch the boat in a narrow space with the floats retracted and extend them once in the water.

One new feature on both the Astus 20.2 and 22 models is that the tubes (crossbeams) are decoupled. This means that the sliding system actually uses 4 overlapping tubes. They were designed this way so the floats can now slide out further to increase the overall beam of the craft. This means the new models have even more stability and power than the original Astus 20.1.

One desirable feature of many trimarans, including all of the Astus models, is their weight. The Astus 20.2 is a fraction of the weight a keelboat its size would weigh. If you take an equivalent sized daysailer with a keel, it would probably weigh about a ton. That means you need a bigger trailer for it. So now the entire trailering weight goes up to almost 2 tons (for the boat and trailer together). So that means you need a bigger car – like a 4 X 4. Most people here in the U.K. don't have a vehicle this size. If you want a trailerable boat there is a limit as to what our small family cars here can tow.

With small trimarans the weight and trailerability aren't issues at all. You don't need a big trailer for the Astus 20.2, for example. The combined weight of both boat and trailer are just 650 kilos (1430 lbs). This means even small cars, like those here in Europe, can tow these boats. So anyone who wants this boat isn't going to have to change his or her car.

This is actually quite important. Anything that reduces a person's sailing budget is notable these days. If you compare the Astus trimarans to many commercial daysailers then the costs are going to be much lower. You don't have to buy a new car. Nor will a sailor have to pay for added fuel or insurance costs.

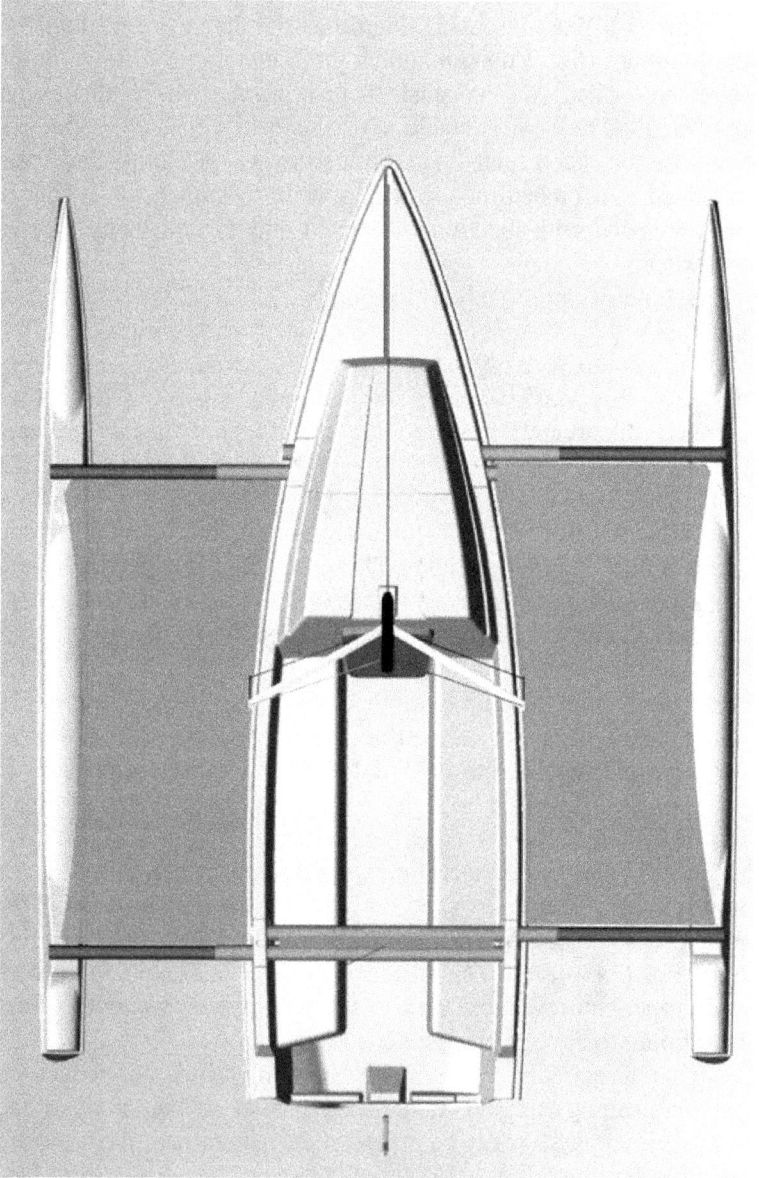

Astus 20.2 rendering

All of the Astus models set up very quickly at the launch ramp too. One key objective for Astusboats was to make these trimarans very easy to use. While these sailboats *are* swift, super-fast performance *wasn't* their main goal. What good is it to have a sailboat that is always a hassle to set up when you want to take it out for a few hours of sailing?

This thinking has now evolved and the Astus 20.2 is offered in two versions: the standard, with a very simple and manageable rig ... and the sport, with a bigger sail area and upgraded fittings. A beginner can buy a standard Astus 20.2 and sail in total confidence, then upgrade to the sport rig to spice up their sailing as they become more experienced.

Our webpage currently links to a video featuring a sailor setting up his Astus 20.1 all by himself. He is able to take the boat from trailer to water in just 12 minutes. He isn't really rushing around either. The biggest part of getting the boat ready to go sailing is raising the mast. This is done while the boat is still on the trailer. After that is finished the boat can be put into the water.

"Room In The Cockpit"

The rig on the Astus 20.2 boat is relatively simple. There are temporary shrouds used to hold the mast laterally while setting it up. And all parts are quite light too. So it doesn't take much effort to raise everything up. When the shrouds are in tension then the mast is where it should be. You then take the gennaker halyard and attach it to the cleat on the foredeck to keep the mast up. Then you tie the forestay to its chainplate. You tension the rig at the same time. You don't need to tighten the side shrouds at this point because the entire rig is tensioned with the forestay.

There is a little more rigging involved with the Astus 22 because it's a slightly bigger boat. The 22 takes about half an hour to set up for sailing. The biggest difference in the rigging for the 22 is that the upper shrouds attach to the floats rather than the main hull. The basic principles, however, are the same.

The Astus 20.2 comes in "standard" & "sport" versions

When setting up the Astus 22, you use a pole, angled to the mast, to lift up the mast because it's too heavy to physically lift. You attach the mainsheet before the mast is raised, support the mast with temporary shrouds, and then raise the mast with the tension control.

The boats are all constructed using modern GRP (glass-reinforced plastic). The shape of the hull on the 3 larger Astus boats is narrow under the floatation line. This allows for low wetted surface where it counts. But it's reasonably wide above the floatation line, which creates buoyancy and room in the cockpit. It's a unique hull shape.

In addition, a lot of attention was given particularly to the floats and how they attach to the main hull. If you look at a picture of the Astus 16.1, the mast is actually stepped on the float mount. This means the main hull takes less of the rigging load. The load is distributed across the deck onto the floats. This allows the 16.1 main hull to weigh less. It doesn't have to be heavily structured in order to bear the load of the rig.

We like to say that technically these hulls are "unsinkable." There are blocks of polystyrene foam put inside both the main hull and floats. Before the main deck is glued onto the hulls, these foam blocks are inserted within. These blocks will always work to keep the boat buoyant.

One difference between these blocks and injected foam is that if you should get water inside the hull for any reason then the water would seep below the blocks and then could be removed later on. The polystyrene blocks will not soak up the water. Injected foam can begin to soak up water after a period of time. That will eventually make a boat heavy. This cannot happen with the Astus boats because their polystyrene foam blocks don't entirely fill the spaces inside the hulls.

The biggest point I can make with regards to Astus trimarans is that they've been designed from the ground up to be easy to use. This is true both for beginners and experienced sailors alike. Even though these boats are very accessible to new sailors they're still very rewarding for experienced sailors to sail. When you learn how to sail an Astus trimaran you're going to enjoy it because these boats can be quite fast yet feel safe and manageable.

The 20.2 model particularly illustrates this. This newer model now offers 2 different rigs. The first rig is what we refer to as the "standard" rig. It features about 20 square meters of sail. It's very simple and doesn't even have a boom. All of its controls are simple too. The 2nd rig is what we call the "sport" rig. It features about 24 square meters of sail area and does have a boom. It also offers additional controls including backstays and a mainsheet traveller so the sheets can be adjusted for increased performance.

It's easy to go from one rig to the other. The standard rig is great for a beginner or even somebody who has never sailed before. The boat's performance using this rig will be nice and easy. It will be hard for a sailor to get into trouble with the standard rig. After a sailor becomes more confident, all he or she has to do is change to the sport rig. The 20% greater sail area on the sport rig creates a more powerful boat.

In force 3 winds the standard sailing rig would allow a good sailor to reach about 8 knots of speed. With a sport rig you're looking at a minimum of 10 knots of cruising speed. Heavier winds allow a standard rigged boat to achieve knot speeds in the mid-teens. And with a sport rig, somebody who knows how to sail can see their boat hit close to 20 knots.

"A Number Of Options"

The biggest difference between the Astus 20.2 and Astus 22 trimarans, of course, is their size. The 20.2 is essentially a true daysailer. It's a smaller boat, and therefore a bit easier to handle than the bigger model. It does have a small cabin, which extends the possibilities of what you can do with it. And it also offers quite a bit of storage for its size. There is room for a porta-potty inside the cabin too.

The 20.2 isn't intended for extensive cruising, even though there are some owners who use it for that purpose. I've got a friend who camped out on his Astus 20.1 with his wife and small daughters for 3 weeks. He slept with his wife in a tent over the cockpit and his children slept in the small cabin.

The Astus 22 is two feet longer than the 20.2. This allows it to have a sizeable cabin with 4 berths and a little galley, with a small stove and sink inside. So with the bigger boat you're really at the place where you have a true small cruiser. It offers more comfort in that regard. So if a sailor wants more space then they would be more attracted to the 22.

Astus 22 at dock

If you go to my website (**www.exaqua.co.uk**) you will be able to see photos of all the boats, including interior cabin shots of both the Astus 20.2 and Astus 22 models. You can even see one picture of a whole family dining inside the 22. Those pictures will offer a good comparison of the room inside each boat. Four persons can sleep inside the Astus 22 cabin. It includes a V-berth and 2 single berths for either adults or children.

The Astus 22 is a slightly more powerful boat than the 20.2 as well. It utilizes winches to control its sails, which are larger than those on the smaller model. So a good sailor can really make lots of adjustments when they're out on the water.

In terms of overall performance, the Astus 22 is probably somewhat equivalent to the performance of the sport-rigged 20.2 model. But in stronger winds the 22 will have a distinct advantage. It sails better overall in bigger seas. It's a bit heavier and features more buoyancy. So it will perform better and be quicker when the winds really pick up.

Astus 22 features a more sizable cabin

Another distinguishing feature of the larger Astus models is that their deck layout puts a lot of emphasis on the cockpit area. The 16.1 can comfortably carry up to 5 adults. And the 20.2 and 22 models can carry up to 7 adults without any problem inside their cockpits. I sold a 20.2 model to a guy who had just sold an 8-meter cruiser. The guy was amazed that the cockpit area of the 20.2 was bigger than the large cruiser he had just sold.

Astus has paid a lot more attention to the outside of its boats than the inside in terms of comfort. You're going to be on the outside sailing most of the time. So that is where they made extra space. And since these boats don't heel, you can securely seat 3 persons on each side of the bench seats (on the larger Astus models).

Astus Trimarans with tents

More Small Trimarans

When you compare the cockpit sizes of the 20.2 and 22 models, they're going to be basically the same. The extra space on the Astus 22 really goes inside its cabin. The cabin of the Astus 22 is actually twice as roomy as the Astus 20.2. But in terms of daysailing, both models allow for 7 adult passengers to comfortably enjoy the ride. As a matter of fact, I sailed an Astus 20.1 this past August with 4 adults and 6 children on board the boat.

The pricing policy of Astusboats is geared towards providing their customers with a number of options. Most people who buy these boats are on a budget. This includes customers who like to do some customizations themselves. In other words, some customers purchase the options Astus offers and others don't. For example, one customer might purchase the seat cushions Astus offers with its models. But another customer may prefer to get their cushions somewhere else.

The Astus production boatyard isn't large. It's small enough that the boat builders actually take pride in being flexible with the customers in order to try and deliver each boat according to a customer's individual needs. For example, they make several different galley options available to each customer. (You can see photos of these various options on our website). One boat may include a sink. Another boat may not have a sink inside the cabin but an electrical hookup instead. A customer may also ask for certain custom things to be done on the boat. Astus always tries to offer competitive quotes for such additional work.

The level of comfort a sailor wants is probably going to determine the choice between an Astus 20.2 and an Astus 22. If you have 2 families, both with 2 adults and 2 children, and one family really wants a high level of comfort then they'll be attracted to the 22. But if the other family is primarily interested in a daysailer that allows them to do some camping, then they'll be perfectly happy with the 20.2. There are many sailors that set up a tent on the trampolines of the 20.2 and enjoy it.

An Interview with Pascal Guignabaudet

A sailor's budget may also influence their decision. There is quite a difference in price between the 2 boats even though they're both going to offer good sailing performance overall.

I have one customer who owned an older Astus 20.1 model and he sold it so he could buy a new Astus 22. When he had the 20.1 he managed to sleep 5 people on board his boat at one time. But since he got his bigger boat he told me, *"Now I can take some more friends along with me."* One weekend, he took 2 families sailing with him aboard the 22. There were probably 10 persons on the boat during the trip. But he was able to put 2 tents on the trampolines to accommodate everybody.

....

For more about the Astus Trimarans visit
http://www.exaqua.co.uk
Contact information for Pascal Guignabaudet can be found at this website.
* Photo credits -- images courtesy of:
Astus 14.1: *VDesign*
Astus 16.1 photos: *Nautical Trek*
Astus 20.2. rendering & photo: *Perspective Yacht Design*
Astus 22 1st photo: *Laurent Sevar*
Astus 22 2nd photo: *VDesign*
Astus with tents: *Nautical Trek*

Chapter 3

An Interview with
François Maillette

Owner, Maillette Engineering
Designer of the MF 18
& Kolibri 23 Trimarans

I've sailed since I was about 10 years old. I took some sailing courses and much of my first sailing was done on a small dinghy model called the *"Optimist."* But I soon started wanting my own boat.

My family lived on a modest income, so I knew that if I were going to get a sailboat of my own I'd have to build it myself. So I began looking at all kinds of boat plans and kits. I continued to sail small dinghies at a sailing club for the next couple of years. And then, when I was 13, I drew out the lines for a wooden boat with a V-shaped bottom.

I was able to get a hold of some building materials and actually build the boat I'd drawn out in the basement of my parents' house. I put an ABS plumbing tube on it for a mast and a very cheap sail using a polyethylene tarp for a mainsheet. I sewed it together using my mother's sewing machine. That was my first boat.

When I got a little older I designed a 13-foot trimaran. I made it out of cheap plywood with no epoxy. I acquired sails from an old skiff and built a wooden mast and crossbeams for it. This turned out to be my first multihull.

Another trimaran followed soon afterwards. I used the floats from my previous boat and built a new 16-foot center hull. I constructed it using a tortured plywood technique with very thin plywood. This is the way some Tornado hulls have been built. So it offers a light solution when using wooden materials.

After completing my studies in naval architecture at the Institut Maritime du Quebec, I built a very good 17-foot trimaran out of plywood and epoxy. It also had aluminum crossbeams and I bought an old catamaran rig to put on it. I consider this boat to be the first really reliable trimaran that I'd built up to that point. (That was about 1990).

During the 1990s I studied composite materials and how they can be applied to naval architecture. I got involved in engineering design competitions where teams were required to design and build racing canoes made with lightweight concrete. My teams even won a few of those.

My thesis paper in graduate school was entitled, *"Caractérisation expérimentale d'un matériau composite à fibres courtes et orientées aléatoirement,"* or, *"Experimental characterization of a composite material with short and randomly oriented fibers."* The paper included materials common in modern boat building, with an emphasis on keeping costs down. My Masters Degree really helped me acquire the theoretical knowledge to design better boats using composites.

After completing my studies even further, I began designing a boat I called the *"Kolibri 19."* (There is a picture of this boat in a pamphlet that readers can receive from me through my website). And then I designed a boat called the *"Akila 19."* When I originally designed the Akila, I attempted to create a planing center hull. I combined elements from the shape of certain skiffs and other multihulls to this new model. The Akila 19 turned out to be more like a very small cruiser, although it could also be used for racing.

I built the first Akila 19 myself. I really enjoyed building it and then testing it on the water. (I have to stop building all of these boats myself, however, because my basement is getting full). ☺

As you can see, I like trimarans. I generally regard them as being more seaworthy than catamarans. I think this is true of both the larger multihull vessels and the smaller crafts. Trimarans can be great sailboats, whether large or small.

I'm not sure why catamarans are more popular than trimarans today. It may be simply because Hobie started making their popular beach cats in the 60s. Prior to that, I think there may have been just as many trimarans in the multihull community as there were catamarans.

I found a very old book at the library a couple of years ago. It was written sometime in the 60s. It showed all kinds of multihulls in production at the time. And for multihulls under 20 feet, there were the same number of trimarans as there were catamarans.

There may be a resurgence of small trimarans in the near future though. When you look at companies like Weta and Astusboats in Europe, you are seeing boats that may offer a glimpse of what may come in the way of small multihulls.

"A Brand New Design Called MF 18 Trimaran"

I tried to take what I'd learned from the Akila 19 and develop its concepts further in a brand new design called the *"MF 18."* The basic goal I had in mind for the MF 18 was being able to compete against F18 catamarans. It's a true *racing boat*; it's not for leisurely cruising.

More Small Trimarans

The MF 18 is a sport trimaran that is built in foam and carbon fiber and I built a prototype in 2006. The main difference between this design and the Akila 19 is that the hull on this newer boat features more planing capability.

The MF 18 is a small but very high-tech boat. I don't think I'll offer it in plan form. I know homebuilders who could build it. But it would be very challenging. When you talk about using female molds and carbon-fiber sandwich construction, then you're really moving beyond the level that amateur builders want to go for a boat this size. The costs in both time and money will probably make buying a production model more attractive. I really think it's better suited to be a production boat at some point in the future.

I modified the boat a little bit in 2008. The mast and crossbeams were moved back a little after a Tornado carbon rig was placed on it. It's a *very fast*, sporty looking boat now. The boat features a radical planing shape for its main hull as well as a folding system for the crossbeams.

Sporty looking MF 18

I discovered that having a boat like this means you don't need a lot of wind in order to make a boat fly. This boat starts to plane in 8 knots of wind, even when going upwind. I look upon this distinct feature as an innovation because I wanted to achieve something new that hasn't been done before. So I would almost define the MF 18 as a skiff with 3 hulls.

Trapezing on the MF 18

Sailing in 15 knots of wind in the MF 18 for an hour gives its sailors a real workout, just like sailing an 18-foot skiff would be a very physical experience. One great advantage is that you have the stability of the floats. But the boat has a very wide 17-foot beam. After each tack the sailors have to move to the opposite side. So they hang on the trapeze while running across the beam to windward.

A sailor can have the fun of planing while still enjoying relative stability in the MF 18. The boat isn't going to quickly tip over, like one has to be concerned about when sailing a cat. The

MF 18 does not ride like a train on a track, as most beach cats do. The downwind amas sometimes dig into the water, but the planing hull sort of makes it respond as if you're sailing on a Laser skiff. The behavior of this boat is almost like a cross between a skiff and a catamaran. It's very unique.

The faster the boat goes the *easier* it is to steer. When you're planing on the water the feeling is completely different than what you feel on a typical catamaran though. I built this trimaran to compete against racing cats its own size.

MF 18 is built to compete against cats of similar size

Those high-tech racing catamarans, such as the F18, are especially popular in Europe. They're very fast. When designing the MF 18 trimaran, it was my intention to create a small multihull that might even be faster than those cats. I took every bit of knowledge I had about design and put it into this boat. Then I put the best materials and the best rig that I could get for it (the Tornado rig) onto the boat. So I have quite a bit of my own time and money in this boat. The result, however, is quite amazing.

If you take the MF 18 and race it against any catamaran of the same length then it will compete. It may even be a bit faster downwind than many of the cats because of the boat's planing hull. In light winds I even have a small advantage because the wetted surface area of this trimaran is smaller than the catamarans. In medium winds, when the cats lift up on one hull, then they will have the advantage. But in high winds (above 12 knots) this trimaran will again be faster than most of the cats.

I don't know of any other trimaran that has been designed quite like the MF 18. There are some small trimarans that possess various aspects of my boat, such as the Magnum 18. But they aren't designed for pure racing so they're not as radical as this design.

"The Kolibri 23"

I designed the "**Kolibri 23**" a few years ago. I constantly receive inquiries about this boat from around the world. At the time of this writing, however, a model of this boat hasn't been built yet. So there are no pictures of the boat in action.

I created this design in response to the request of a French magazine. They asked me to design a sailboat for them that would be shown in a special issue of their publication. My design was compared to others' models in an issue that discussed boat designs of the near future in this new millennium.

The first thing that is somewhat unique for a trimaran this size is the wave-piercing aspect of all 3 hulls. I'd just finished designing the Kolibri 19 and its hulls feature the same wave-piercing hulls concept. So I adapted this feature onto the bigger boat.

On a small trimaran that is about 23 feet or less, the weight of the crew is large when it comes to the entire displacement of the boat. Simply putting bigger floats on smaller trimarans isn't always a good solution for increasing the boat's performance. My MF 18, for example, uses the weight of the crew to balance the boat and give it stability.

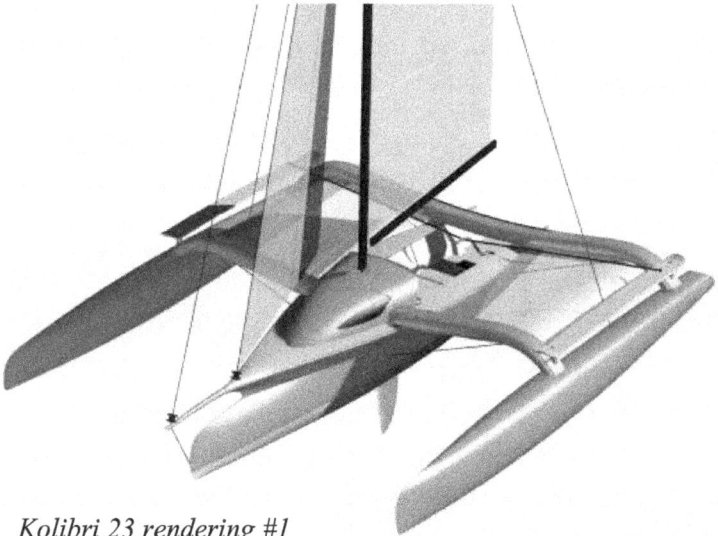

Kolibri 23 rendering #1

With this wave-piercing concept, you must start with a trimaran of a certain length and adjust the sail area to the function of that length. I tried stretching this boat out lengthwise so that it would be more seaworthy. Then I reduced the sail area of the Kolibri 23 because the hull volume was reduced towards the front of the boat. Its sail area is slightly less than some other boats of similar size. And its hulls are also very light in order to be efficient with less sail area.

An Inverview with François Maillette

The hulls are designed in such a way that they shouldn't slam into waves at all. This will especially help the sailboat when it's going upwind in choppy conditions. But even with this being the case, the volume of the floats is still around 150% of total displacement. They're quite big for this boat. But they're not *too* big. After all, a sailor isn't going to try and sail on one float.

When you reach a certain length on small trimarans you need to decrease the displacement of the floats. I've tried a number of float sizes with my small trimarans. The float volume on my Kolibri 19 was moderate. Then I tried very large floats on the Akila 19. But on a small boat like that, sailors aren't going to be flying along primarily on the floats. So I lessened the volume of the floats on the Kolibri 23 to where I think it's about right.

I know that builders often look at using catamaran hulls as a cost-saving solution when building a trimaran. But I don't think that catamaran hulls should be used for hulls on a trimaran in most cases. The floats on a catamaran aren't designed to be submerged as much as the floats on a trimaran will be forced to go underneath the water. In my opinion, it's better to use properly designed amas for a tri.

As a designer I always think about these things in terms of structural issues. The chain plates that attach the crossbeams to catamaran hulls should be changed in order to adapt them to a trimaran because the loads are going to be greater. So a builder needs to keep that in mind if they try to adapt catamaran parts to fit a small trimaran.

The hulls for the Kolibri 23 are designed to be constructed with a PVC foam sandwich core and fiberglass skin ... the same as a Farrier F22. The curved shapes of the hulls offer a boat of superior performance so I don't recommend this boat to be built in plywood. Light weight is essential too. So a homebuilder can get this using a sandwich construction without too much trouble.

It's more complicated to build a boat like this than to build one in plywood. But with a small cruiser like this you're probably at the point where it's worth the extra effort to learn how to build using composite materials. After a builder learns how to make their first vacuum-bagged panel then they're on their way to building a boat using modern materials. A lot of builders are scared of building in PVC foam sandwich. But once they try it I think they'll find out it's not too difficult. I've built lots of boats using lots of different materials and I don't think most builders will think it's a big deal after learning how to do it.

A plywood kit boat, for example, can save a builder lots of time at the beginning of the construction process. The builder will see a hull in front of them in just a few days. But after that, all of the interior taping has to be done, which becomes very time-consuming. Plywood boats usually require extensive framing inside. Then the builder is going to have to tackle the exterior finishing. So in the end, I really don't think there is going to be a lot of difference in time and effort when comparing a boat constructed in PVC foam sandwich against a plywood boat. After you add in the time it will take for fairing and painting, I think the amount of time required to build both kinds of boats is comparable.

A boat built in PVC foam and glass is going to cost a bit more. But the end result will be lighter and the resale value will probably be higher than for a wooden boat because a lot of people are afraid a wood boat is going to rot. It's hard to know for sure, but the perceived value of a wooden boat may be less than one built using modern PVC foam construction. So I think foam sandwich construction is a better investment in the long run.

There are a couple of different ways a homebuilder can construct the crossbeams for the Kolibri 23. It all depends upon what the builder wants. They can build simple crossbeams that bolt onto the hulls. Or they can make a folding system that is somewhat similar to what they might see on a Farrier trimaran. But that would be more expensive.

The materials used to build the crossbeams include some high-strength, yet lightweight carbon. A builder will construct a female mold and then create each beam within it. The crossbeams will have somewhat of a U-shape and then a plate will be attached to both ends that bolt the beams to the hulls.

The mast for the Kolibri 23 was designed especially for this boat. A builder will take my plans to a mast maker and have them build the mast for them. I do not recommend trying to use a mast from even a large catamaran for this boat. It's not very safe. I know some guys who have built small trimarans using hulls from Tornado catamarans and then used the Tornado rig to sail it. That will work. But you have to realize that a catamaran rig isn't designed to take the kind of load a trimaran is going to place on it. A small trimaran with a wide beam can have twice the load on its mast that a similar sized beach cat might generate. So I think you should use a mast that is especially designed to handle the righting moment of a sailboat.

The mast for this boat is a specifically designed rotating mast. It should be good for both cruising and a bit of racing. There is a company called *Forty Carbon*, which sells carbon masts relatively cheaper than other mast makers. Their masts are made with filaments rolled around a mandrel. They can make a less expensive mast using this technique. It's a less pricey way to go while still getting a good mast. It won't be as high-tech as you will get from a strict pre-preg carbon mast maker. But it's a good compromise for a builder who wants to save some money.

"Light Weight And Low Wetted Surface Area"

The Kolibri 23 does offer some interior accommodations. I wanted to design a trimaran that would allow sailors to go further on extended cruises more comfortably. I'd taken my wife sailing for a few days during the past few summers on the Akila 19 down the St. Lawrence River. We sailed and did some camp-cruising. We found the 19-footer to be a little too small for this though. We both would have liked a little bit more comfort. So the Kolibri 23 would meet these needs.

I designed it to be an ideal small trimaran for up to 4 adult sailors to go sailing. The boat will be very comfortable for 4 sailors to take on a cruise. The cabin offers 2 comfortable berths inside and 2 sailors could sleep in a tent on the trampolines. The cabin size is also ideal for small children to play inside and also provide shelter in case of a thunderstorm.

That being said, most sailors will probably go camp-cruising for a few days when there is going to be nice weather. So instead of trying to fit everyone inside the cabin I thought it was more practical for this sailboat to feature a larger cockpit and a smaller cabin. There is plenty of room for a couple of sailors to sleep on the trampolines of this boat.

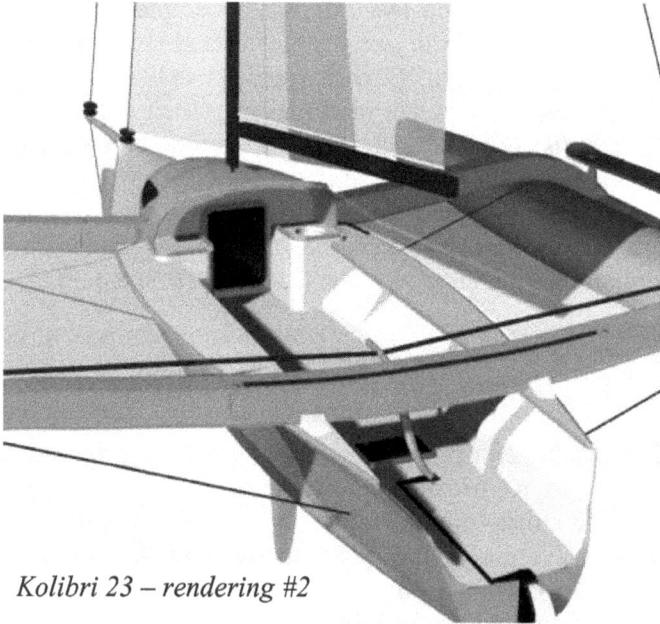

Kolibri 23 – rendering #2

The cockpit on this boat is very roomy. It will be comfortable enough for sailors to ride in together when under sail and there is enough room to be able to use a small cooking stove and do all of the things required on a camping excursion. It's big enough that sailors can set up a table inside it and then throw a tarp over the boom above their heads in order to get out of the sun for a few hours if they want.

The Kolibri 23 will tend to be fast because it's light. It should perform very well for a sailor who knows how to handle the boat. With 1 or 2 people on board, they might see close to 20 knots going downwind when using a screecher. In medium winds this boat can probably cruise up to 15 knots without any difficulty. In lighter winds the boat will offer comfortable sailing in the range of 8 to 12 knots for those on board.

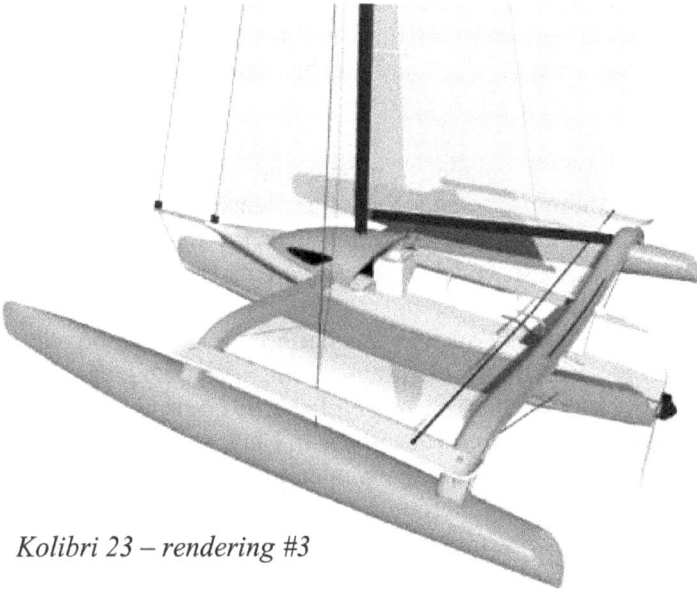

Kolibri 23 – rendering #3

When you look at the Kolibri 23 renderings, you'll note there are optional *"hiking wings"* at the end of the crossbeams. This is a comfortable way for sailors to hike out onto the amas without having to sit on wet trampolines or floats. These hiking seats will let passengers sit about 12 inches above a float when sitting on the windward ama. You could even set up a panel on these wings for back support. Equipment like this can go a long way into making long hours on the water more comfortable.

The sailor who is attracted to the Kolibri 23 will be somebody who wants to spend their time doing some camp-cruising along coastal areas. The boat is ideal for this. But if you look at the boat's light weight and low wetted surface area it will also be a good boat for local racing events. This will sort of make it a multi-purpose boat.

I don't think it's a good idea to put a large cabin on a small trimaran like this. Since the interior accommodations are somewhat limited, the boat doesn't suffer from being overweight. The wind drag against the main hull is going to be at a minimum. The boat actually looks a little bit like a racing boat for this reason.

On the other hand, the cockpit is large enough to accommodate a couple of people and there is enough cockpit room and trampoline space to offer plenty of space for camping. The cabin doesn't end up taking over the main hull so there is plenty of open space where it can be conveniently enjoyed in the cockpit area.

Small trimarans such as this one are ideal for going out on the water for a few days of camp-cruising. Not long ago, my wife and I took the Kolibri 19 out on Lake St Louis and Lake of Two Mountains, near Montreal. It was in May, at the beginning of the sailing season, and we really wanted to take this little trip.

We decided we were going to go even if the forecast called for gale force winds. I was confident that I could handle the boat, even in high winds like that. All I'd have to do is put a little reef in the mainsail and furl the jib. The thought of dealing with 30-knot winds didn't bother me. So we went out on the lake and all kinds of catamarans were attached to the shore because in 20 knots of wind they would have been in survival mode.

An Inverview with François Maillette

In our small trimaran, however, we were able to easily control the boat, even when things got real gusty. It's nice to know we didn't have to panic when one of the floats went under water. You have plenty of time to adjust your sails and fix that situation in a small tri. It was actually fun for us to be out on the lake that day with just a little piece of sheet on the mainsail. My wife and I got out on the wings and eventually sailed to our sailing club on a day when other club members would never have come out onto the water. It's times like that I really enjoy the benefits of sailing a trimaran.

……………………………….

For more about François Maillette's trimaran designs and other marine and structural engineering services visit **http://www.mailletteingenierie.com/**
Contact information for François Maillette can be found at this website.

Chapter 4

An Interview with
Tony Grainger

Owner of Grainger Multihull Yacht Design & Creator of the Trimaran Now Referred to as "Moving Finger"

*(**Editor's Note:** Tony Grainger requested that the interview questions posed to him be included as part of the reading for this chapter.)*

How did you get into sailing?

I started sailing VJs (Vaucluse Juniors) as a kid. They're a 12' long dinghy class, built in plywood and completely decked. They had curved wooden "leaning planks" that we used to slide from side to side as we tacked.

We sailed VJs off the beach at Terrigal, north of Sydney on the Australian east coast. They were totally unsuited to the open ocean conditions there. Later on, Terrigal became a popular venue for Hobie cats. But at that point I'd moved on to surfing.

I've always had a strong interest in art and design. I was interested in the design of sports cars from a very young age, but I guess it was the combination of my love of the ocean and a pure interest in design that steered me towards drawing boats.

Can you give me a quick synopsis of your business?

Our work at Grainger Multihull Yacht Design primarily involves creating both racing and cruising multihulls -- up to about 20m LOA. They're mostly sailing boats but we do a few power cats as well. We've been in business since 1986 and my design work in Australia has come primarily through a combination of word-of-mouth and magazine coverage. Our overseas work comes mostly through our web site.

"Born To Run"

My first design was a 26' (8m) trimaran. I had previously built a 33' Crowther trimaran for myself and was living on board. I had some ideas for how the technology could be advanced and embarked on my own design. The design I came up with was the 26-footer.

I published this design in a local yacht club magazine and a Melbourne businessman saw it and asked me if I would build one for him. I did and we called it *"Born to Run."*

Its first race was the ANA Regatta in Melbourne, which is now known as Audi Race Week. Born to Run was an outstanding success on the course from day one, and we took the boat on the race circuit on the Australian East Coast.

From there, it went on to win other races and wide honors throughout Australia. I started getting inquiries from others who wanted racing trimarans. That's how my business started growing.

An Interview with Tony Grainger

The larger part of my work in those first years was focused on smaller racing multihulls. Since then, however, my business has grown and expanded to include a full range of boats that include cruising catamarans, workboats and charter boats.

We specialize in custom designs, but we also do design work for production builders. The process is very similar to the way somebody hires an architect to design a building and then goes out and hires a contractor to build the structure afterwards.

In your opinion, what is the biggest appeal of sailing small trimarans as opposed to sailing other types of small sailboats?

The biggest appeal of sailing small trimarans in the under 30' size range, as opposed to sailing other types of small sailboats, is that you can have reasonable cabin space compared to a cat and better performance than a monohull of similar size. A small trimaran is also easier to trailer than a cat, especially if it has a folding system.

"Driven By An Objective"

Can you discuss the design process (for you) a little bit, and how you approach a new small tri design?

The first step is the idea in your head - the "vision" if you like. The whole process has to be driven by an objective, whether it's just to create something visually appealing, or to achieve some performance goals, or to combine a whole raft of design objectives. In most cases there are a number of design parameters that have to be met and it's usually the art of integrating these features that determines the successful outcome for the project.

I use software called *Alias Sketchbook Pro* for preliminary sketching and concept drawings in my work. Sometimes I also use it to create preliminary presentation drawings for clients. We then use a program called "*Maxsurf*" for the surface modeling work. And then we use a software known as "*Vectorworks*" to create working drawings, 3D renderings and to produce cutting files and 3D models.

"*Moving Finger*"

One of my early designs was a boat now called "*Moving Finger*." It has had several different owners, who each gave it a different name. The boat has previously been referred to as, "*Riverside Oaks*" and "*Dux Nuts*."

*The model first called "Riverside Oaks" ... **

Moving Finger was designed in 1986. Riverside Oaks was her sponsor at the time, so that was the name originally given to this boat. She was designed for a gentleman named Graeme Bird.

Graeme had been inspired by the performance of *Born to Run* at the Hamilton Island Race Week event that year. He was the manager of a company based in Sydney, Australia called *ATL Composites*. ATL Composites manufactures resin systems for applications in the marine industry, among others.

The design parameters for Moving Finger were quite clear. It had to comply with the IYRU Rule Book (International Yacht Racing Union) at the time, which is now known as the ISAF (International Sailing Federation). It also had to be trailerable and had to be fast.

... then referred to as "Dux Nuts" *

The IYRU Rule Book, referred to as "the blue book," included all of the racing rules and design rules for sailboats that participated in its races. It represented the worldwide standard for racing boats.

The guidebook required a particular volume for the cabin of Moving Finger. Even though it was a racing boat there was a headroom requirement that had to be fulfilled over a certain area of the cabin for accommodation purposes. I designed the form of the cabin top around this rule.

There's a double berth forward in the cabin and another berth under the cockpit. This trimaran, however, isn't really designed with cruising in mind. The access to the cabin is quite difficult and you wouldn't want to spend a lot of time in there. There is room though for a porta-potty, small cook stove and refrigerator inside the cabin.

The boat is built from strip planked Durakore and epoxy. The hull laminates are glass but the beams are built from plywood and carbon fiber.

Durakore, which was developed by ATL Composites, is made out of endgrain balsa with timber veneer. It comes in an 8'x 4' panel, and was an excellent material for strip planking. The thickness could run anywhere from 3/8 of an inch to 3/4 of an inch.

Durakore was a very popular boatbuilding product in Australia at the time. It was used on all sorts of boats, including cruising cats that were up to 50 feet in length.

Moving Finger was created to be demountable, and therefore trailerable. But it probably takes about two or three hours to set up the boat for sailing and then a similar amount of time to be broken down to put back on the trailer. The time it takes to set up and break down just depends upon how much experience the crew has had with the operation.

Now referred to as "Moving Finger"

The crossbeams on this boat attach to (and detach from) the main hull with a series of locking pins. When the boat is trailered the floats stay attached to the crossbeams. The floats fold in on the trailer and the beams stick up in the air.

Back in the mid-1980s, sailors used to control their small tris mostly from the cockpits. They'd move out onto the trampolines once in awhile to steer and work the sheets but there wasn't really a nice rigid place out on the tramps to support the sailors so they could properly sail the boat. People have developed all sorts of solutions to this problem since then.

You see sailors out of the cockpit and on the windward float regularly today. But when I designed this boat for Graeme he came up with the idea of using 2 aluminum tubes with trampoline mesh wrapped around them in order to create a comfortable seating area between the floats.

We called it the "*bus seat*." It simply ran fore and aft between the beams and allowed the crew to get their weight outboard and provided a good helming position. The bus seat was Graeme Bird's idea and it turned out to be a real winner.

"The Line Honors Trophies"

Moving Finger was a custom design and if we had the same design brief presented to us today the outcome would be quite different. Our more recent designs, such as *Essential Eight, Trilogy,* and *ST7* all feature relatively larger floats.

More Small Trimarans

As the designs have progressed we've focused on wide beam overall, good beam clearance from the water, and higher float buoyancy in order to be able to drive the boats harder. In order to do this, we've had to sacrifice some ease of trailerability, but the focus on these design parameters has paid off in race results.

Over the years, our boats have consistently taken the line honors trophies in races such as the Australian Trailerable Multihull Championships, the Queensland Multihull Championships, the Bay to Bay, the Marlay Point Race, the Lock Crowther Memorial Regatta and the Surf to City. Our designs currently hold line honors titles in all of the above races and most of them on handicap as well … although not always trimarans … some of these races have been won by cats.

The following was sent to Tony Grainger from Graeme Bird, who recalled some of his sailing experiences with this small trimaran (italics mine).

Hi Tony,

One story I remember is during the last race of the Hamilton Island Regatta. Verbatim (*a very well known 40' Racing Tri designed by Lock Crowther*) was about 0.5K ahead, with about a 10K broad reach to the finish, in 25 knots and choppy seas. We closed and all but caught them by the finish in conditions that were ideally hers.

We were small enough, however, to use the seas to the best advantage and were sailing the boat to the max, with Gregg sitting on the outboard to help keep the bows out, Brownie (*a legendary 18' skiff sailor from Sydney*) on the kite and myself steering the boat down, up, around and all over the waves in a wild, wet and exhilarating ride.

Another (*event took place during*) the first Mooloolaba Regatta Race when, after a light run out of Moreton Bay, we had a huge lead on Born to Run that we subsequently lost on the tight reach and light slog to the finish. (*There was* a small seaway and a dying breeze).

I remember when you came down to meet us you had this theory worked out on how each design had its strong points, and Born to Run (*was*) a better tight reaching boat … only to learn (*later on, that*) we had folded our rudder shaft and had steered the last half of the race with our outboard leg -- with considerable loss of performance.

Another time, in the Mooloolaba Regatta, was when a maxi tacked in front of us on a lay line to the top mark. I just pointed up and sailed over the top of them, rounding the mark ahead, to the disbelief of the crew on the weather rail of the maxi.

I feel Riverside Oaks (*Moving Finger*) was/is a very successful design for what we knew at the time. I had ideas for another improved version after the first season, with many of the ideas you mention in the interview … more beam, buoyancy in the floats, bigger rig etc. It's been fun remembering these times and events again. Thanks for copying me on this.

    -- Graeme

....

For more about the "Moving Finger" Trimaran visit **http://www.graingerdesigns.com.au/**
Contact information for Tony Grainger can be found at this website.
* First 4 photos courtesy of Bob Ross (of ***Australian Sailing*** magazine).

Chapter 5

An Interview with Graeme Delaveau

Designer of the Nicky Cruz Trimarans

My father started making canoes when he was about 7 years old. He paddled in creeks as a boy, fit a sailing rig to his canoe and loved it so much that he eventually got into sailing dinghies, P class through to T's, eighteen footers and Mulleties. When I was 8 years old, dad built a 28-foot Wharram "Tane" catamaran so he could take our whole family out sailing with him. Being a young kid, that was magical sailing for me.

Dad was a schoolteacher. So every holiday and most weekends our family would get out on the water. I'd often get home from school on a Friday and mom would have boxes of food and clothing already packed so we could all go down to the boat and head off. It was fantastic.

We enjoyed some nice voyages in that boat. Our family of 5 sometimes went out for 3 weeks at a time. One funny thing about this was that mom couldn't even swim. She did very well on that boat though.

About the time my father built his catamaran I got interested in building model boats from plans. I'd save up my pocket money and send off to England for small model boat plans -- usually around 25 inches in size. The biggest one I ever built was a meter long; it was a catamaran. That made me quite adept at building boats from simple plans. But those models actually gave me a very basic understanding about how to build boats as a kid.

As we all got a bit older Dad wanted to race his catamaran. And we did end up racing it against other catamarans, trimarans and keel yachts in mixed fleet racing. All of this gave me a good knowledge of sailing and racing while growing up, especially with multihulls that could perform very well.

That catamaran would just "take off" when conditions were right. It would even go to windward well. I enjoyed sailing on that boat until I was about 17 years old. I got into surfing as a young adult, and then other things began taking up my time.

"A Piver Nugget"

When I got into my early 20s I wanted to go surfing down the New Zealand coast. I wanted a boat that I could anchor off a bar and catch the 6-foot waves that formed just off of the bar breaks. So I started looking for an old, dilapidated tri.

I ended up purchasing a Piver "*Nugget*" trimaran for about $600. I rebuilt it, and then put it back into the water and daysailed, raced and cruised with it. I owned it for 8 years and it turned out to be a powerful little boat. It got me to thinking about how much could be done with a trimaran that was around 24-25 feet in length.

 www.SmallTrimarans.com

An Interview with Graeme Delaveau

The Auckland Harbour is a beautiful and nice sheltered area to sail and cruise with lots of islands to explore and run to if the conditions get too wild. I found the Nugget to be very seaworthy and I was able to sail it to the many islands around Auckland. We'd go out in that 24-foot Piver trimaran for days at a time and even up to two weeks at Christmas. We really enjoyed sailing it. It really didn't take much to power it up. The boat performed really well when the wind got up to around 18-20 knots.

My sailing experience as a boy provided me with a bit of seamanship that helped me understand how to get the most out of the Piver Nugget. When the wind picks up and the sea starts getting choppy you have to reduce sail and get things under control. But I learned a lot about how to handle rough conditions in that Piver. There were times when we sailed back to Auckland in very nasty weather after being away on the weekend ... sometimes into 45-knot winds and big seas. My Piver would just knife right through it. We'd reef down and never got into any trouble on that boat.

I rode out several storms along ocean beaches on my Nugget during those years. We'd set our anchor amid 3 to 4-meter waves plowing onto the shore. The Coast Guard would come along side us with spotlights and ask, "*Can we throw you a line and tow you off this coast?*" We'd reply, "*No, we're okay. We're all fine!*" We'd just ride out the storm and the next morning it would be over. Everyone on board would just dry out the interior and we'd head back home.

There were quite a lot of Piver Nuggets built around Auckland in the 60s. We'd see them around Auckland's waters all the time, sometimes 30 nautical miles up the coast. Mates regularly went out sailing and had lots of fun on those small tris. I remember one Nugget quite vividly from back then; it was named "*Magic Bus*." It had diamond-shaped floats and was well known by lots of sailors at the time.

"A Stunning, Absolutely Mind-blowing Performer"

My opportunity for yacht design came after I got into boatbuilding work. I'd built some boats that were over 40-feet long. It was good work but it didn't really hold any interest for me personally because I wanted to build nice slender hulls. I'd gotten a taste of multihull forms from my prior years. I just couldn't get the inspiration I derived from slender hulls from the big, bulky launches I was building at the time.

I managed to become part of a yacht design course in Auckland. But my lucky break came when I was introduced to a very talented adaptable retired yacht designer in Auckland named Brian Donovan. The course had been a challenge because it was all empirical stuff ... theory galore. But then Brian came in and was very practical in his teaching approach. It really helped me. He taught me things covering everything from fishing boats to live-aboard sailing yachts. The largest boat he'd designed was a schooner that measured 109-feet on deck.

Brian was actually looking for somebody to pass his knowledge on to. I was very interested in that because my goal was to design and build my own boat. I spent my spare time learning all I could about yacht design for the better part of 5 years.

About a year before Brian passed on, I finished my first design, the Nicky Cruz 28-foot trimaran. I'd taken it to him and said, "*Brian, what do you think?*" He went over my plans for about 10 minutes and then said, "*It looks fine. It'll work.*"

That's what I needed to hear. So I went out and bought all of the materials and built it. The Nicky Cruz 28 turned out to be a fantastic success and I've never looked back.

My inspiration to design and build a 28-footer came from my desire to do longer distance racing. A Nugget-sized boat isn't suited for that kind of thing. I needed a boat that could carry a lot more weight and perform a lot better than the Nugget, even though that Piver tri had been a good 24-foot performer. I wanted a boat that would get me to places faster with a higher degree of comfort.

Nicky Cruz 8.5 Performance Coastal Cruiser (28' LOA)

The cabin on that first Nicky Cruz trimaran ended up quite a bit bigger than I'd originally anticipated. I ended up with 6' 2" of headroom in there. That boat also featured a modest rig. But it was still capable of reaching 22 ½ knots of speed in the right conditions.

Nicky Cruz 8.5

An Interview with Graeme Delaveau

It was a stunning, absolutely mindblowing performer in light winds. And when the wind blew up, and the weather got a bit nasty, the sailboat was still able to perform really well because its beam and displacement afforded it good handling as a true sea boat. During one race, I completed a run where I covered 126 nautical miles in 12 ½ hours. The interesting part about that, though, was the last 14 miles of that race took 4 hours. So I'd covered the first 112 miles in just 8 ½ hours.

The performance of this boat proved a lot of things to me. It showed me that it's possible to build a boat that is really light, but also allows for easy and comfortable performance-oriented sailing. The Nicky Cruz 28-footer weighed in around 1 ton. That was considered to be quite light for a trimaran its size at the time. She proved to be a true performance family cruising trimaran.

The original Nicky Cruz, along with the smaller trimaran models I designed afterwards, was made to be permanently moored. They're not trailerable in the sense that they're made to be quickly taken apart, put on a trailer, and then towed somewhere where they can be quickly set up to go sailing again.

However, the demountable aspect of these boats comes from the fact that most owners build them in their backyard. They build the boat as separate components and then take them all to the beach where the boat is then assembled and moored in order to go sailing. Several years later, the owner may want to take the boat home for maintenance. So at that point the boat would be taken apart, put on a trailer and then taken to the spot where it'll be worked on.

One of my goals has been to provide homebuilders with high performing multihulls at a modest cost. There are guys out there who've built skiffs, dories and canoes that come to a point where they want a bigger boat. But they still want to build it themselves without spending a fortune.

Nicky Cruz 8.5 Demounted

I've chosen to design boats that can be built with materials such as plywood, epoxy and fiberglass sheathing. Nothing has to be dovetailed with these boats. My boats are designed to be small, light, efficient, economically built cruisers. They offer, however, the type of performance you'd normally see in more technical and expensive boats. I've tried keeping the size of them down though because keeping costs and construction time down for homebuilders has always been a big goal of mine.

Nicky Cruz 7.6 Sports Weekender (25' LOA)

"The Nicky Cruz Explorer"

My newest design here, however, is meant to be truly trailerable. I'm calling it the "*Nicky Cruz Explorer*." I got the idea for this design from sailors who've said they were looking for a simple and trailerable trimaran that's even smaller than the ones I'd already created.

To be honest, I didn't think I was going to be able to produce a design like this that would be particularly useful. But I got the sketchbook out and started playing around with some ideas that included what I'd want from a trimaran of just over 20-feet in size.

More Small Trimarans

Even though this is a relatively small boat there was a lot of thought that went into it. I didn't want to produce a boat that a sailor is going to put lots of effort and work into building and then quickly grow out of it. In my opinion, if a homebuilder goes through all of the hardship of building something that turns out to be a mere daysailer then it's not worth the effort because you can go out and just buy boats like these. There are little tris, Hobie cats and literally hundreds of day boats that already fit the bill.

In my mind, if a guy is going to bother with setting up a workspace, buying materials and spending the hours building a trimaran, the project needs to be worthwhile. The problem, of course, is that many small cruising trimarans can take years to build.

On the other hand, you wouldn't want to finish building your boat, put it into the water, and then feel like it wasn't worth the effort because the boat is so small you can't take anyone out on the water with you. That's the way I approached this new model. I wanted the end result to be able to be used for many things: daysailing, overnight camping or even going out for a week at a time (for those who are well-organized).

The Explorer is designed with enough freeboard and volume in the main hull to carry a reasonable load. (I actually took a few ideas for this new boat from the Piver's Nugget design). This sailboat will also feature an inexpensive hinging system that allows it to be quickly and easily folded and trailered.

I have worked out a simple way to create an efficient hinging system that takes the compression loads required. I settled with a system that uses pins to lock the crossbeams in place when they're fully extended and opened up. The same pins will lock the floats down alongside the boat when the system is in a folded position. This will make it unnecessary to use lifts or supports for the floats when setting up the boat to go sailing. After trying to get the maximum amount of beam possible using such a system, I think this model is going to be quite a stiff little performer.

An Interview with Graeme Delaveau

The average homebuilder can probably have this hinge system fabricated rather inexpensively by either a sheet metal worker or company. The sailor can order their own bar stock, angle iron in stainless steel, have them cut to length and then take everything, along with my plan's drawings, to a sheet metal worker in order to have the parts welded together. Four complete sets of these hinges should only cost around $800. If the homebuilder knows how to weld, then they'll be able to build this hinge system themselves.

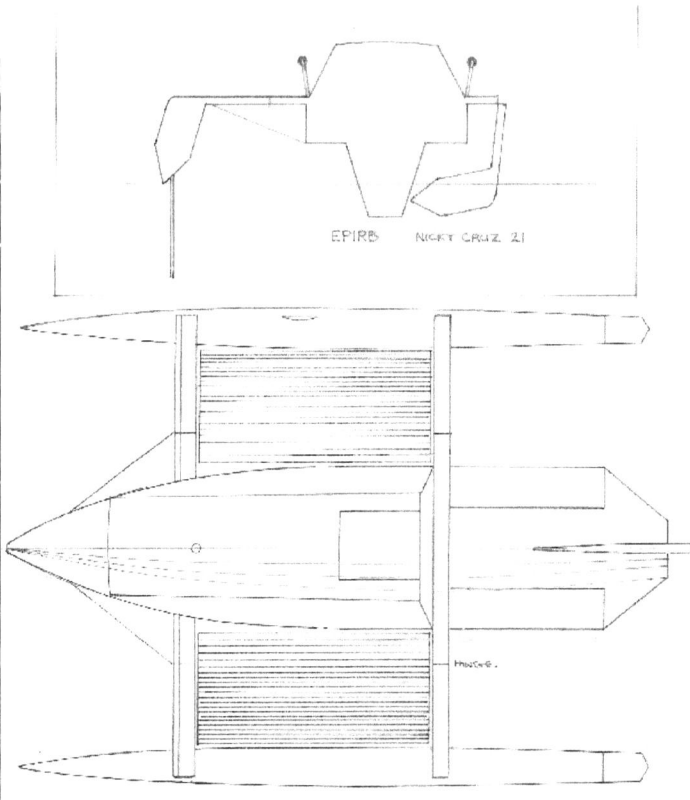

Sketch of new "Nicky Cruz Explorer" with hinge system

More Small Trimarans

The Nicky Cruz Explorer is going to offer quite a good volume of hull. The main hull has 5 feet of headroom and 5 feet of beam. This allows for a double berth in the cabin. There is full sitting headroom in this berth, so you don't have to hunch over inside it. And no horizontal maneuvering will be necessary to get into the berths either, as in many small boats.

The cockpit is of decent size too. It'll be a comfortable cockpit to sit around in. There'll be plenty of storage underneath the cockpit also. A small child could even sleep under there. The cockpit has been kept open at the stern so you can step up onto the boarding platform after taking a swim and walk right into the cockpit without any obstructions. There are even generous trampoline areas for lounging around on and positioning crew when under sail.

I've kept the daggerboards out to the floats just to make sure the interior space is uncluttered and useful. The daggerboards will be canted in the floats in such a way that they'll offer dynamic lift when sailing. Their location will also add to the stability of the sailboat too.

When constructing the hulls, a builder will create the chine skeleton and then place cut plywood pieces onto the various sections of the chine. The process will primarily involve cutting flat sheets to be glued, screwed or nailed onto the timber skeleton. The floats will be constructed of 4-mil ply and most of the main hull and deck will use 6-mil ply. All 3 hulls will be sheathed with 6-oz fiberglass and epoxy resin.

It'll be fairly simple construction. Only minimal beveling will be required ... just some off the stringers and chines. There'll also be some cedar on this boat. Cedar is a nice, durable, lightweight wood to use for the hull framing.

When it comes to the type of plywood used in my boats, I've fallen in love with marine-grade meranti plywood. It's beautiful material. Meranti is a strong, lightweight and durable hard wood. It's certainly one of the lightest weight plywoods that are available for purchase and it's naturally very durable. Okoume is also great plywood for boat construction.

Meranti can be exposed to water (though not good practice) and it'll resist rot on its own for years. I've still got scraps of meranti ply lying underneath my house from when I built my Nicky Cruz 28-footer back in 1990. Whenever it rains those pieces get saturated with water. I've gone underneath my house and got pieces of ply and put them outside in the sun for a day to dry out. Aside from looking just a bit "grainier," the stuff will come out looking just like it did back in 1990. Meranti ply is widely available. It's grown in places like Indonesia and Malaysia. But regardless of what kind of marine plywood used, a builder should always use top grade materials that have minimal flaws in them.

Another economical feature will be the motor used on this boat. The Explorer will be able to use a 5-horsepower outboard. The boat should really boogie with only a 5-horse attached to it in calm water.

In my opinion, a builder who works on this boat about 3 days a week (weekends plus an accumulative amount of hours during the week) could actually have the boat ready to go into the water in about 6 months.

A resourceful builder should be able to build this boat fairly economically, especially if they search for bargains. A builder should always search around for various suppliers and then get several quotes from each one. For example, you can call trampoline manufacturers directly and get quotes. See if they're willing to part with leftover materials or overstock for less. The same thing can be done for sail material.

"Terrific Light Wind Performance"

One feature I'm really enthusiastic about on the Nicky Cruz Explorer is the rig. The rig is essentially a 3 ½ inch spar. It's a pivoting, rotating rig supported at the top by a forestay and shrouds. I've put a decent rig on this boat without overpowering it. But this boat should handle very nicely because of its nice displacement capability.

Nicky Cruz Explorer (21' LOA) sketch #2

An Interview with Graeme Delaveau

I like having a boom vang on the Explorer (and all trimarans of this size). I consider it essential. I've tried to keep this rig low and there isn't room for a traditional boom vang, so I've opted for a strut that attaches to the mast and goes down to the boom. When you're sailing and have to ease off a bit and have to dump the main you can just let the mainsheet go and the boom won't sky up. A sailor can lose control when things like that happen. Sailors often need to de-power quickly because of a sudden gust of wind. If you're going along nicely in 12 knots of wind and then get a sudden gust of wind that overpowers you, just let that mainsheet go to bring the boat under control. Without a boom vang the boom will just rise up and make it harder to control.

This rig will also feature a furling jib. You can set the headsail up, for example, on a Harken furling system (**http://www.harken.com**) or one from any number of other manufacturers of furling systems. But I know Harken has a good one for this boat.

I've designed the mast sections for this boat in such a way that homebuilders can either make them themselves or get them made. The builder can do much of the work if they're competent with a drill and rivet gun. I've tried to keep things simple enough for most builders that they can even make the fittings themselves -- if they want to. Keeping things simple is the main thing. A small boat like this doesn't have to be overly engineered or expensive.

This sailboat will offer terrific light wind performance because it has a planing main hull. The floats are deep V-shaped, so they have fairly minimal wetted surface. And if the wind picks up then this tri will have enough righting moment and stability. The daggerboards inside the floats will provide lift upwind as well.

I anticipate speeds attainable up to 20 knots under the right conditions. That kind of performance all comes with experience though. I had my Nugget going 15 knots at times and that was quite a heavy boat. But that only came after lots of experience sailing it.

This boat will nicely accommodate up to 5 adults when daysailing. You can actually grab some friends and take them along in order to push the boat a bit harder by putting them out on the windward float. If you're sailing downwind and want to go really ballistic then you can even fly a gennaker!

"The Beauty of Having a Small Trimaran"

What I personally like about the Nicky Cruz Explorer is the fact it can be trailered and built really inexpensively even though it features a folding system. We kept the mast as short as it can be so that a single sailor can rig the boat on his or her own; they should be able to *"walk it up."* The rig is also easy to handle in that it'll be easy to trim and depower because of the nature of the mainsail and the reefing system.

I think the Explorer is going to have a wide-ranging appeal for all sailors. A complete novice could even sail this boat … they'd just have to sail it reefed to start with. Since the boat has a furling headsail, a novice sailor could just sail with the main at the first reef until they get to really know the boat.

In this sense, it'll be a very forgiving, easy boat to sail – just like the Piver Nugget was. My old Nugget was actually a very forgiving boat. It's a matter of confidence really. A beginning sailor should really think about how much sail they want to have up.

This boat is going to be well behaved at the helm and will tack beautifully so it'll do what you want it to do. If you do ever have to pull off some kind of radical maneuver then the Explorer will respond to the helm quickly, which will make it a safe boat.

The furling jib is convenient too. The headsail isn't very big to begin with but a sailor who is confident is always able to sail with more canvas.

The beauty of having a small trimaran like this is it offers a sailor the ability to sail with ease and confidence. Then you can pack up your camping gear, fishing rod and supplies and head off to some island. When you arrive at a nice sheltered bay you can drop the anchor, dangle your line in the water and enjoy the beauty of your surroundings. In all of the traveling I've done over the years there is nothing quite like being able to do that. It's precious to be able to enjoy the simple pleasures of life with a boat like this.

………………………………….

For more about the Nicky Cruz trimarans, including the new *Nicky Cruz Explorer*, visit
http://www.delaveaumultihulldesign.com
Contact information for Graeme Delaveau can be found at this website.

Chapter 6

Ed Horstman's Tri-Star 18 Trimaran

(**Editor's Note:** *This short chapter features Ed Horstman's 18-foot Tri-Star model. Although Ed did not participate in a formal interview, he did spend a few minutes on the phone with me and shared a little about his background and the Tri-Star 18 specifically. He then sent me some additional written materials in the mail, which he wrote. Ed encouraged me to use some portions of those materials verbatim within the manuscript of this chapter. This chapter combines the information gathered during my phone conversation with Ed and the previously published materials he gave to me. I then forwarded a preview of this entire chapter to Ed in order to secure his approval for publishing).*

Ed Horstman's love affair with boats began in his home state of Montana. He was born near a small dam in a town called Bigfork. As a child, his grandfather showed him how to carve boats, which he then pulled along the shore waters of Flathead Lake.

Ed built his first boat in high school wood shop at 13 ... plus the wood bowl for "mom." It was a 13' 6" kayak. He then used it to navigate and fish most of the rivers and lakes of northwest Montana.

In 1953, while stationed in Texas as a helicopter mechanic in the US Air Force, Ed found an old *Aeronca Chief* airplane sitting under a tree and looking for an owner. The Aeronca Chief only cost $600, but to a staff sergeant in those days, that was a lot. So Ed borrowed $400 from his buddies (in turn for their usage). He completely rebuilt the NC 9052E while learning to fly her. The Chief was later sold to help pay for college.

Ed enjoys working with his hands, including building and rebuilding. He recently began rebuilding a 1942 PT-17 Stearman, the biplane that most of the pilots of WWII learned to fly in. These planes were often used later for dusters and sprayers. The woodwork and fabric have a correlation to boat building. Ed is going to enjoy making the first flight once it's completed. It will compare to the enjoyment of launching his first boat and the 4 subsequent ones he built of his own designs.

Beginning in 1961, Ed's participation in the multihull movement began with research about trimarans. At that time, he was working as an aeronautical engineer for North American Aircraft Co. in the wind tunnel design group on the B-70 supersonic bomber program. When Ed finished his research, he designed the Tri-Star 40 and built a scale model of it for testing.

The sailboat model worked great, in that it showed where and when improvements should be made. Ed then spent 4 years working as an engineer at Hughes Aircraft Co., while building Tri-Star 40. What he'd learned with his model was later verified in the performance of his full size 40-foot trimaran after it was finished.

Incidentally, Ed first coined the word *"Tri-Star,"* and applied for a registered trademark. He had difficulty showing overseas sales at the time however, and Lockheed Aircraft Company announced a contest at the time to find a name for their new "tri jet." The contest winning entry, of course, was "Tri-Star." Since Ed was into sailboats, and Lockheed was into aircraft, the 2 businesses decided to share use of the *Tri-Star* name. There are now many businesses and products that use this name.

Ed's 50-foot design, "*Aries,*" was the first trimaran to be certified by the Coast Guard for passenger-hire back in the 1960s. The Coast Guard had gone back and forth with him regarding the safety specifications because Ed had placed his I-beams in a different location than where the Coast Guard thought they should be. For evaluation, Ed provided data that proved his point. He was able to satisfactorily prove the ama clearances were quite sufficient for safety and performance.

When it came to his 65-foot design, the Coast Guard officials couldn't believe the Horstman trimaran only used half an inch of skin. *"How can you make a safe 65-foot boat with only a half-inch of skin?*' they asked. As an engineer, Ed once again provided the numbers and data needed to make his case.

According to Ed, many larger multihulls during the 60s just weren't the sailing vessels they are now. They weren't able to *"point to weather"* when sailing. Nor could many "*come about*" either.

"The First Tri-Star 18"

The first Tri-Star 18 was built by the designer. And a gentleman who had first built a Tri-Star 48 design (later sold to a charter business) built the second Tri-Star 18. (The man went on to build one of Ed's 35XR models after that).

Ed said the charter business that purchased his client's former 48-footer used it for 10 years in Hawaii. They told him it was the best boat they'd ever had. *"They'd take it out of the water for servicing for a couple days each year and then it was ready to go again for another year."*

The new Tri-Star 18's builder was a PhD professor at the University of Washington and he became one of Ed's best friends. Ed said this fellow really liked speed.

The professor had a wife and children who also wanted to go sailing. So he asked Ed to design a small trimaran that could be used by all of his family members to go out sailing around Lake Washington. Ed thinks his friend's wife must have really liked the Tri-Star 18 because when his friend eventually sold the boat his wife was *very* unhappy about it.

The Tri-Star 18 Ed built for himself is featured in the Tri-Star brochure and on his website. It includes pictures of the 18-footer being built. Ed took these photos during the construction phases of his Tri-Star 18.

Tri-Star 18 (photo courtesy of Ed Horstman)

After building the first 18-footer, Ed needed a trailer for it. So he went to Seattle in order to look at a 25-foot trailer that was being advertised for sale to see if he might be able to purchase it for his new boat. As Ed was conversing with the guy who owned the trailer, the fellow told him the following story, *"You know, we were out fishing in Lake Washington last fall. It was very cold. Yet we came across a guy in the water. The fellow had a life jacket on and we could tell he was in danger of freezing to death. So we picked him up out of the water and asked him what happened. He said he'd been out sailing in his 18-foot trimaran but had a 12-year old boy with him at the helm. He'd gone up to do something on the sail and the kid jibed the boat and the fellow got knocked into the water. The kid at the helm in the boat didn't know how to tack back to him. We just happened to be there at the right time and retrieved him."*

Tri-Star 18 on trailer (photo courtesy of Ed Horstman)

Ed laughed as he recalled the story. He knew immediately the guy who fell into the water had to be his friend. And thankfully, the story ended well. The professor, however, never shared his experience with Ed about falling out of his little trimaran.

"Outsailing The Other Boats"

The Tri-Star 18, like all of Ed Horstman's boats, is fitted with a sloop rig. Ed was sure other sailing configurations just wouldn't perform as well for this type of boat. *"The two sails available from the sloop rig are all that's needed to make most boats efficient,"* he said.

More Small Trimarans

Ketch rigs were tried on some of his bigger boats at one time. They sailed fine but slower. The ketch rig's best point of sail is downwind because of the sail area that 2 masts can put up. But even though they were easier to handle, it turned out the ketch rigs just weren't better than sloop rigs on Ed's trimarans.

Tri-Star 18 (photo courtesy of Ed Horstman)

Plans for the Tri-Star 18 include the I-values for its mast (which records the strength it's supposed to be). This allows the boat builder to go to a mast manufacturer and show they need a mast section that offers the I-values specifically designed for the boat. In Ed's opinion, most boat builders should be willing to go out and buy an aluminum mast for their trimaran.

He does offer a drawing for homebuilders if they want to make their own mast out of spruce. But Ed encourages homebuilders not to make their own mast anymore. In his opinion, it takes too much time.

Ed Horstman's Tri-Star 18

He did point out that a builder can build a wooden mast -- if they enjoy woodworking and can obtain mast grade spruce. And he also suggested that if a builder does make their own wooden mast then they shouldn't varnish it because it will just need to be varnished again in another year. He believes wooden masts should be painted instead of varnished because the end result will require less work to maintain.

The Tri-Star 18 can be set up and taken apart by a single sailor. It also has fixtures that allow for the crossbeams to fold easily.

The early plans for Tri-Star 18 called for its amas to be "folded up" over the top of the cockpit. But later on, they were revised to allow for the amas to fold up or down beside the main hull. The plans include instructions on how to do all of this.

Ed said that when he sells a set of plans to a homebuilder, he doesn't expect to hear from them because the plans are very detailed. His plans come with full sized patterns, instruction sheets and a photo sheet of all construction steps.

The amas for this small trimaran can be made from either plywood or foam fiberglass. Using metal, such as aluminum, would be expensive. And in this designer's opinion, it would get the boat out of proportion (weight-wise) for a small boat like this.

Ed encourages new builders to build even small tris like the Tri-Star 18 in foam/glass rather than wood nowadays. The reason is because he still owns his own Tri-Star 18, which has sailed for a number of years on Flathead Lake, and doesn't enjoy the added maintenance that comes with a wooden boat.

He keeps his 18-footer inside his hangar so he doesn't have to wipe it out periodically due to rainwater getting into the bilge. A Tri-Star 23 Ed also owns is fiberglass … and can stay outside without any concerns about water getting into the boat. This notes the challenge of trying to protect a wooden boat left outside, even if it's built with epoxy. It's also the main reason why Ed now encourages builders to construct his boats in foam if possible. (He provides prospective builders with an estimate of the time it will take to build the Tri-Star 18 in wood *or* foam).

More Small Trimarans

The 18-footer can sail with up to 4 adults on board. Ed figured that if a power boater could take an 18-footer out with 4 adults then his 18-foot sailboat should be able to take out 4 adults too. Although he was quick to point out that the Tri-Star 18 wouldn't go super fast with 4 people aboard. He was confident, though, that it would still allow its sailors to enjoy a nice ride in a stiff breeze. He once wrote that the Tri-Star 18 featured a "hull shape that is still outsailing the 'other' boats."

"If a sailor only puts 2 people in the boat it'll go a lot faster," said Ed. He noted that if a sailor knows how to sail, and the conditions are right, then the Tri-Star 18 should easily be able to perform consistently in the 15-knot range. *"If you're outside of a harbor and get into choppy water, the 18-footer is small so it's going to bounce around a lot. So it's more realistic to say you can sail at about 10-12 knots without any problems."*

All in all, Ed felt the Tri-Star 18 still offers small tri enthusiasts plenty of fun sailing opportunities. It's a boat that can be built to enjoy the wind and spray of a good day sail.

. . . .

For more about the Tri-Star 18 Trimaran visit
http://www.edhorstmanmultihulldesigns.com
Contact information for Ed Horstman is available on this website.

Chapter 7

An Interview with Paul Dawson

Designer of the Predator Trimarans

I was born in England but my family moved to New Zealand when I was 2 years old and I was introduced to boats there. We moved to Fiji when I was about 8 years old, and while there, I started racing in a 'P'class, which is a New Zealand designed, small sailing boat. As I grew older I got into *Moths*, which is a very well known small sailboat that fit me well at the time.

My family eventually moved to the continent of Africa, to a country called Rhodesia (now called Zimbabwe). Zimbabwe is a landlocked country but I still wanted to sail. So I found a worn 18-foot Cross trimaran, which I was able to fix up and sail, mostly around the lakes in that country.

When living in Zimbabwe, a trailerable boat was the only way to go because I had to drive in order to access large lakes or the sea. There were few affordable boats available. The rates of duty were very high and it cost a lot of money to import products like this. I knew I could find cheap catamarans and I knew I could build something that the catamaran rigging and hulls would attach to.

The thought occurred to me afterwards that other sailors might be interested in acquiring this type of trailerable trimaran. This whole concept is now a personal passion of mine. I knew that if I didn't pursue my dream of creating this sort of sailboat then I'd regret it for the rest of my life.

The last boat I had in Zimbabwe was a trimaran that took me about 4-5 hours to put together each time I wanted to go sailing. The main hull was from the mould of a Kellsall Tonga Trail catamaran and the amas were cut down Piver Mariner amas. I'd tow it down to Mozambique or up to Lake Kariba and then spend the next few hours putting it together so I could go out on the water. It sailed beautifully but all the work required to set it up made it less practical as a trailerable boat.

When the political situation in Zimbabwe became untenable, I left to start a new life in Australia with my wife and two young children. I came here thinking that it would be an ideal place to begin working on an idea for a small trimaran design that I had in mind.

The Idea Behind the Predator 17 & Predator 21 Trimaran Designs

I'd seen a lot of guys build small tris by adapting catamaran rigs and floats to their boats. But nobody had ever designed a system that was what I refer to as a "universal" design.

By universal, I mean one that used a central hull that could utilize a wide range of catamaran rigs and hulls in order to create a trimaran. For example, there are a number of trimaran designs that can use a Hobie 16 or 18 rigging and floats. But that's all they can use. The original *Tremolino* is one such design. It used a Hobie 16 rig and hulls.

There are heaps of trimaran designs around that can adapt beach cat parts for use. But none of them were designed to be a production boat that could utilize a wide variety of sizes when it came to beach cat rigs and floats.

Predator 17

One reason I conceived of this concept was because I would've liked to have something like a Farrier or Dragonfly at one time. But they're expensive boats. I took note of the many beach cats that are just lying around unused. I thought many sailors might like to use those as a good starting point to put together a very desirable small trimaran. So my goal became creating an original tri design that can use just about any available beach cat.

I ended up with the concept of using a central hull with a lateral beam that allows for adjustment between various sizes of differing beam attachments. This allows for a variety of catamarans to be attached to the central hull in order to create a trimaran configuration that works pretty well.

More Small Trimarans

The challenge has been doing something original that nobody else had ever attempted to do before. But I thought, *"Well, why not make a go of it?"* My personal expertise has come from sailing, reading, looking closely at every boat or other multihull design that I could find and watching other people do things in highly practical ways. I've tried out many different things over the years and learned from those experiences.

Predator 21

There are some broad categories of catamarans. The little ones are about 14 - 16 feet in length. The Hobie 14 is one such cat this size and many other manufacturers built models that length in order to compete with them. One version of the Predator tri features a 17-foot main hull (the **"Predator 17"**). The Predator 17 is designed to be an open daysailer. It will ideally accommodate either 4 adults or 2 adults with 2 children.

It utilizes the rigging and hulls from catamarans in this 14 - 17 foot size range. The 16-foot cats are somewhat big and powerful for the Predator 17 but that size is great for anyone who wants to race his or her boat.

For catamarans in the 16 to 21-foot size range, I've designed a 21-foot main hull (the **"Predator 21"**). This was the design I originally conceived of because a central hull that size will accept the larger catamarans I originally had envisioned using in order to create a trimaran in the 20+-foot range.

The Predator 21 features a cabin in the front that can either be closed or left open. Its size doesn't intrude upon the cockpit, where most sailors are going to want to be when sailing. But it's big enough to let anyone who wants to get out of the sun for a while go inside or even lay down. There is also ample room for a Porta Potty and supplies for the trip.

It sports a king-sized V-berth in the front of the cabin and is set up for a genuine camping type of experience. It's not really an enclosed cabin with a kitchen, sink and all of that. You can fit those kinds of camping appliances inside if you want. But the cabin has room enough to where owners can customize their own camp-cruising trimaran in the way that best suits their particular needs.

More Small Trimarans

When it came to designing the unique hull shape for both Predator models, I had to first think about what each one needed to do. Then I thought about what I wanted them to look like.

The main hull for the Predator 17 was designed around certain parameters. I needed this model to be a good match for a 14-foot catamaran. It needed to fit onto a 14-foot cat trailer. The

102

Predator 17 needed to have sufficient volume and space for 2 adults and 2 children. I needed to make sure it had a large, family-friendly cockpit. And I wanted it to have sleek looks and the potential for great speed.

I wanted the Predator 21 to be adaptable to most, if not all, 16-foot plus cats. Its hull needed to offer the potential for speed. But I also wanted it to be a great family boat.

The decision between which of these 2 versions a sailor chooses will depend, in part, upon what category of catamaran an owner either already has or plans to acquire. The sailor will then match it with a particular Predator model in order to custom build his or her own trimaran.

"A Pretty Massive Cabin"

Most small trimarans in the size range of the Predator 21 feature cabins. Even trimarans that are a bit larger, including those in the 24-foot range similar to the Trailertri 720s from years ago, can only realistically accommodate 2-3 people in their cabins. Most families include 4 or more persons. And if 2 couples want to go sailing together then there will still be 4 individuals that need accommodations. But if the trimaran's cabin is enlarged to comfortably make room for 4 persons then its cockpit becomes much smaller.

I think the ideal solution is to put a big tent over a larger cockpit area in order to sort of combine the small cabin's space with the cockpit's space. If you do that then you can have a pretty massive cabin on a relatively small trimaran like this. This solution allows the same boat to be both a relatively open daysailer and a very comfortable camp-cruiser at the end of the day.

An Interview with Paul Dawson

The cockpit area in the Predator 21 is about 2 meters wide by 2 ½ meters long. There is enough room to sleep 6 persons inside the Predator 21 when the tent structure is set up and connected to the cabin.

The framing to make this camping enclosure, which encompasses the cockpit area, is made of aluminum. It comes with each boat. At the back of the Predator 21 is a *targa* or stainless steel arch, which is mostly used as a place where the boom can rest. This arch is also used for the tent structure. (This framing structure is like the framing used on yachts produced by Hunter Marine - **http://www.huntermarine.com**). So the essential framing to make the tent is a fundamental part of the Predator 21's design. As far as the actual tent goes, we can make the tent for a customer or the buyer can hire somebody else to do it if they feel they can get better pricing.

Tent material can snap around the framing at the end of the boat, across both sides of the cockpit, and then onto the cabin at the other end. That is one option. Another option, which makes the tent structure even bigger, is to extend it out to the outer hulls. That will cover the trampolines on each side and create a huge camping space underneath. I don't know if there is one "best" way to create the camping enclosure. It all depends upon how a customer wants to set up his or her own sailboat.

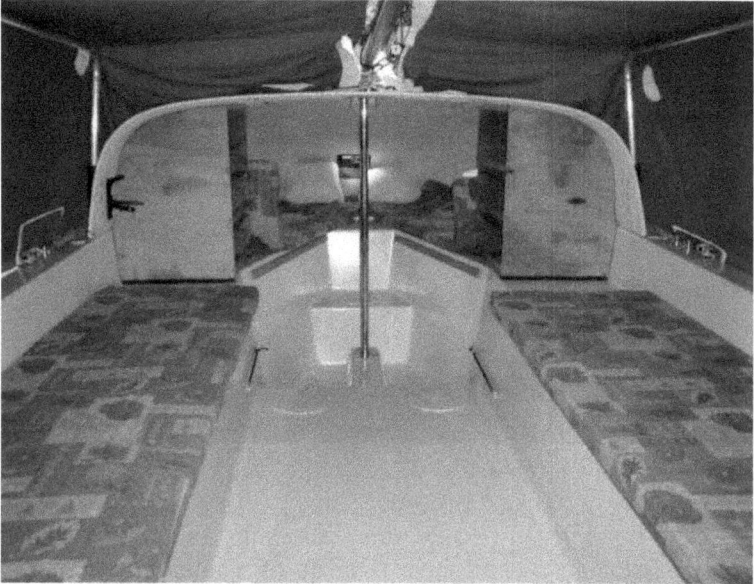

I've even used big woven polypropylene tarpaulins (or groundsheets). These are found in most hardware and camping shops. They were tied to the outer hulls in order to make a huge tarp covering over the boat. The whole setup only cost about $50. Other customers have used a type of bimini that folds down over the top of the cabin and across the top of the boat. I arrange it so customers can decide what they want to do.

An Interview with Paul Dawson

"Utilize Different Sized Catamarans Into A Universal System"

When somebody orders a Predator model, I provide the main hull, sliding beams, trampolines, mast step, targa arch and jib tracks -- all assembled and fitted. The customer gets everything they need to bolt on cat hulls and attach the rig. A customer will also need to know what catamaran they'll use with their Predator so I can make a mast step that fits the mast they're going to use.

There is one location for the mast step on each boat. The main adjustment for each individual boat is made where the floats attach to the lateral beams. The hulls can be moved either forwards or backwards in order to adjust for their size. And the volume of these floats will primarily affect the righting moment of the boat when sailing.

If you've got Hobie 16 hulls attached to a Predator, for example, then you can change the balance of the boat by moving them to where they need to be in order to optimize the boat's sailing performance. Moving the hulls is simply a matter of loosening some bolts and then tightening them up again. It's easy to make adjustments.

The hulls slide out to a fixed distance. But if you want a larger righting moment then you could attach larger floats to the main hull, such as those from a Hobie 21 or Mystere 5.0. That would increase the sailing budget. But the great thing about this system is that if a sailor can afford Hobie 16 hulls right now, and then wants to acquire a larger rig and hulls in the future, then they can do it. And if a sailor ever wants to use their beach cat as a catamaran again for some reason, then they can easily demount it from the Predator and set it up to go sailing in its original form.

The Predator system offers sailors a wide degree of flexibility in these regards. No holes ever have to be drilled in the original catamaran in order to use them with the trimaran configuration. I don't know of anyone else that has created a universal trimaran system like the Predator, which is able to utilize many different sized catamarans like this.

More Small Trimarans

The Predator's aluminum crossbeams can slide in and out, which makes them very convenient to use. In the past, some people criticized this type of system because the beams could jam up if one wasn't careful to slide them in and out evenly. But I designed an articulating sliding system that prevents jam-ups. It's essentially a jam-free system because of the way the beams slide into the tubes.

Both Predator models are easily trailerable. I designed the beam width on the Predator 21 to be 8 foot wide because that is the legal trailerable limit in many states. The Predator 17 beam slides in to less than 8 feet. The trailering width of the Predator 17 will ultimately depend upon the width of the original catamaran.

When it comes to trailering, the Predator 17 is going to be light enough to fit onto the original trailer of whatever catamaran you're using with it. A Predator 21 owner will have to acquire or build a trailer that supports its specific size and weight. Hobie 16

or Hobie 18 catamaran trailers aren't solid enough to carry the Predator 21.

A Predator's mast sits in a roller on the targa bar when it's being trailered. The stays will ideally be attached when you arrive at the boat ramp. To get the boat set up for sailing, you get onto the boat, slide the mast back on its roller and pin it to the base. Then you set up a little tripod, which is supplied to you. You then attach the mainsheet to it and a fitting on front of the boat. Then you get off the boat and go to the front of the trailer to pull up the mast with the mainsheet. Then you tighten everything up. (This is a simple, 1-person job).

The mast stays can remain attached to the main hull on the Predator 21. After the mast is up, you can lower the boat into the water, go park the car, then come back and get into the boat in order to raise your sails.

The hulls are pulled out (extended) using a rope and pulley system. You just pull on the rope on one side and one hull will slide out while you're in the water. Then you use stainless steel pins to secure the beams into place fore and aft on that side. Then you cleat the pulley rope. Then you go to the other side and repeat the process. You can then raise the sails and go from there.

The whole process takes a single person anywhere from 20 to 30 minutes. Pulling the hulls out is about the only additional thing a sailor has to do with this boat that they may not have to do with some other types of trailer sailers.

There is a short YouTube video linked at my site (**http://www.predatortri.com/index.html**) that demonstrates the mast being raised and the hulls being pulled in and out.

Launching the Predator 17 is even easier because it's a smaller boat. All you have to do is sit inside the boat and push the hulls out using your legs and feet and then secure the beams in place with pins. At that point, you can just lift the mast up by hand because the smaller beach cat masts used on this model are pretty light. Then you can tie it off.

The trampolines stay attached to the beams at all times using a sail track and a bit of lacing. If you feel like there is a need to loosen the tramps after the hulls are retracted then you can easily tighten them again when the hulls are extended out again.

"A Huge Amount Of Reserve Buoyancy"

Most sailors who are interested in the Predator tris want to have some idea about their performance level. If the Predator 17 utilizes a small 14-foot catamaran then the sail area will be easily managable because 14-foot cats don't have big sails. One of my customers sails with his wife and 2 small children using this setup. He said he uses a GPS all the time and he's seen his boat hit 14 knots on some occasions.

If you want to race a Predator 17, however, then you could use the rig and hulls from a 16 or even 17-foot catamaran with it. I'm currently building a Predator 17 that is going to use a Hobie 17 cat. I'm not sure how fast it might be able to go … but in my opinion, anything over 15 knots is quite fast for small trimarans in this size range. This matchup is going to produce a seriously fast sailboat under the right conditions.

If you owned a Predator 21 and put a 16-foot catamaran's hulls and rigging on the boat then you wouldn't be using it for racing, but you'd go faster than most monohulls and have a nice easy boat for cruising. When you match the Predator 21 with something like a Hobie 18 then you're probably going to be able to hit 15 knots at times (without spinnakers). But if you merge a Formula 18 cat or Hobie 21 with a Predator 21 then you're probably once again looking at a boat with some seriously fast potential. I don't think it would be as fast as an F-24, but I think you'd certainly be able to make most people's eyes open real wide when you're out on the water. Putting an asymmetrical spinnaker on a Predator 21 is another thing you can do in order to try and reach the top of its performance capability.

An Interview with Paul Dawson

Another reason sailors should be able to have some real fun with this boat is that its hull configuration offers a huge amount of reserve buoyancy, especially in the bow. There is a maximum amount of flair in the front portion of the main hull. Whenever the boat starts going into a wave it just lifts up right out of it.

I designed this hull with the idea that it's going to be primarily sailed in bays and semi-sheltered waters. There are often very choppy waters in such areas. I wanted the Predators to be able to nicely cut into 1 ½ to 2-meter waves. The main hull offers very fine entry at the narrow point and then flairs out to about 2 meters wide. This has resulted in an incredibly dry boat when sailing in these conditions.

One sailor I know recently took out a Predator 21 into breaks that were about 2-meters high. (The breaks turned out to be higher than what he first thought they were). But he was able to get in and out of the breaking waves and stay completely dry in the process.

A Predator tri naturally wants to lift up when it goes into a wave because of the shape of its main center hull. For water to get over the top of these boats and into their cabin area would require a pretty large sea.

Both Predator models have self-drain holes in their cockpits. So in that sense, they're both "self-bailing." Some trimaran designs out there have open transoms that allow water to come into the cockpit and then flow right out the back again. I avoided that feature in my design because I really wanted the cockpit to be enclosed. I didn't like the idea of a child or one's camping gear being washed right out the back of the boat. So the Predators' cockpits are fully enclosed.

If a massively big wave were to enter into the cockpit then you'd simply bail the boat out until the drain holes eventually took over and removed the rest of the water. Any water that comes into a cockpit will ultimately drain out through its drain holes.

"A Very Social Friendly Boat"

The Predator 17 is ideal for 1 or 2 persons to sail in if the boat is set up for racing. But if you want to just putter around and go check out small islands or coastal areas then the boat will comfortably sail with 4 persons aboard. There'll be plenty of room in the cockpit and also space on the trampolines.

The Predator 21 is really only limited by its flotation with regards to how many can go sailing in it. The cockpit can easily seat 3 adults on each side. And then a couple of older kids could, in theory, hang out on each of the trampolines. The weight of that many people on board would obviously affect the boat's performance. But some sailors really enjoy taking out family members and friends for rides.

An Interview with Paul Dawson

The Predator 21 is also a very "social friendly" boat. What I mean is that most sailors will be able to stand up in the cockpit without getting hit in the head by the boom. If you're tall and standing up front next to the cabin then you'll probably have to lower your head a bit when the boom swings. But most individuals standing in the middle or back of the cockpit will be able to stand upright without worrying about getting hit in the head.

I've really tried to design this boat so it's safe, easy and comfortable to use. It's designed to be "family friendly" and enjoyable. You don't want a boom to come across and easily whack kids in the head. And you don't want 3 year olds to easily be able to fall out of the back of a cockpit either. So you might say this boat has been designed mostly with families in mind.

Another unique feature of the Predator 21 is something I was inspired to do by the *Macgregor 26* – a top selling monohull trailer-sailer. The MacGregor 26 has the ability to lower its sails and become a fast motorboat. In the same way, you can lower the sails on the Predator 21 and retract its hulls while the boat is still out on the water. Then you can fire up the engine and it becomes a compact motor cruiser.

More Small Trimarans

If you attach a big motor to the Predator 21, such as a 30 horsepower engine, then when the wind drops or your family has simply had enough of sailing by the end of the day, you can fire up the motor and the craft becomes a powerboat.   You can actually fit a 30-hp 2-stroke motor on the Predator 21 … if you want one that large. The boat will cruise at about 20 knots with its hulls tucked in using a motor that size. It's remarkably stable when you run the boat this way too. And it also allows a family to engage in some water activities, such as pulling rafts, which are typically associated with motorboats.

On the other hand, if you want to use the Predator strictly as a sailboat, then you can simply attach anything from a 3 ½ to 6 horsepower motor onto the back of it and it will get you in and out of the marina just fine. You'll also be able to motor back to your launch area if the wind dies down.

The Predators are ideal for anybody who once sailed a beach cat and then got married and had children. Since most beach catamarans aren't good family boats, the Predators enable the cat's hulls and rig to be converted into a fast, safe, family oriented sailboat.

The Predators are also great boats for somebody that really wants a fast trimaran but doesn't have time to build his or her own … or who doesn't have the money to spend on one of the fancier production trimarans on the market today. A sailor could, for example, buy a used Hobie 17 cat, attach it to a Predator 17, then go racing. And it would cost much less than what most others pay for an expensive production tri.

I normally don't supply any cushions or "extras" with a Predator because sailors can go out and find ideal accessories on their own. That will save them a great deal of money. Camping stores and big super stores have an endless supply of those kinds of things. Production boat companies typically overcharge customers for those kinds of items. I let my customers go out and find whatever products they want to make their boats ideally comfortable for themselves. Why spend $300 for something when you only need to spend $10. The goal is to keep the price down.

An order for a Predator can generally be fulfilled (production wise) in 6-8 weeks. Then it takes about 20 days for a boat to be shipped to another part of the world. My intention is to reduce this time quite a bit with the assistance of dealers who have boats in stock.

I want to offer Predator trimarans to sailors around the globe, including the United States. I'm currently inviting any individuals who'd like to be entrepreneurs and market these tris to contact me. They can become dealers who will represent the company and always have 1 or 2 Predator tris on hand so potential customers will be able to come and see the boats.

Prospective buyers naturally want to be able to see and touch the Predator trimarans and even possibly go out for ride on one. So having Predator models in stock is essential. And I'm open to forming partnerships or types of dealer arrangements in certain parts of the world.

....

For more about the Predator Trimarans visit
http://www.predatortri.com/index.html
Contact information for Paul Dawson can be found at this website.

Chapter 8

An Interview with Eric Henseval

Owner of Henseval Yacht Design & Creator of the "Sardine Run" Trimaran

I've sailed on family owned boats since I was born. We had little cruiser-racer monohulls and sailed from France to England, Ireland, Spain, etc. They were hard sailing trips when I was a young boy, but I was still fond of those navigations.

It has always been my ambition to become a sailor and a yacht designer. I always loved to draw boats. I don't know really why. One thing to note is that both of my grandfathers were architects, and their grandfathers also.

When I grew older I got involved in the boat delivery business and served clients around the Atlantic. It didn't matter what type of boat I was sailing, how difficult the route was or the season of the year. I looked upon those challenges as a test of sailing skills.

That experience helped me gain firsthand knowledge of various types of vessels, including their strengths and weaknesses. After sailing approximately 30,000 nautical miles on about a hundred different boats, including racers and cruisers, I gained some experience about what works and what doesn't. There were some "misadventures" along the way too, including a shipwreck during one of my solo navigations in 1996.

By delivering boats to customers, I was able to sail to places such as Scotland, Madeira, and the Azores. And I was able to make some transatlantic passages by sailing to the United States.

I eventually went on to formally study naval architecture at Westlawn Institute of Marine Technology. Their program really helped me structure my professional knowledge and progress towards the goal I'd had since childhood, which was becoming a boat designer. I think I'm one of the last designers in France to ever learn how to draw boats in preliminary sketches by hand – before learning the 3D computer modeling that is standard today. Drawing things out by hand is an excellent way to visualize a design and think about how to deal with certain ergonomic challenges.

I've worked as a yacht designer for 10 years now and was able to set up my own little design office in 2005. One of my first projects was a little 18-foot cruising-racing monohull called *Kouign Amann*.

My business currently focuses on designing sailboats that make it possible for all types of individuals to go sailing. In other words, I enjoy designing a boat for a particular person; I do not design boats for *myself*.

I work on specific projects by being a boat designer for one unique person at a time. Since every person is unique and needs something different, each project requires me to work within the limits of certain well-defined specifications.

An Interview with Eric Henseval

I got into sailing multihulls when I was about 20 years old. In my opinion, it was good for me to discover multihulls *after* having a large amount of sailing time on various monohulls. My multihull sailing now includes racing in the *Formula 28* World Championship on the catamaran "*Charleston.*" Sailing on high-tech carbon fiber multis was a great experience.

Around the same period, I also sailed on older *Formula 40s*, which were originally developed in France. My crew became fond of navigating those boats around the difficult coast of Brittany. Sometimes we even sailed in the rough seas of Brittany during the winter. It was wonderful.

I got really involved in designing multihulls when I worked at one of the most famous design offices in France (and maybe in the world). It specialized in big racing trimarans. These trimarans typically measure 60 feet and above in length. They're the big tris you often see in the news because they frequently engage in transatlantic races and round-the-world navigations. That design office was MVP-VLP (Van-Peteghem-Lauriot-Prevost … **http://www.vplp.fr/flash/index.html**). This is also the office of *BMW Oracle*, which is participating in the America's Cup Race. It was a dream for me to be integrated into that design team!

There were 4 of us who worked in the office. We collaborated on all of the subjects and engineering challenges in order to complete several big projects. One of the projects I worked on was the 60-foot Trimaran *Foncia*. There is a YouTube video of her sailing on my website **(http://www.hensevalyachtdesign.com/travaux-et-réalisations/les-trimarans-60-pieds-open/**). I also worked on the famous *Groupama 1* and *Groupama 2* trimarans, which included the responsibility of helping to draw up the hulls for Groupama 2. There are a number YouTube videos featuring these sailboats as well.

More Small Trimarans

"The Sardine Run Trimaran"

There is a small, relatively new boatyard here in France, located on the Atlantic coast, called *Sardine Boats* (**http://www.sardineboats.com/**). The owner and main boat builder at Sardine Boats, Mr. Allel Behidj, contacted me about doing a small trimaran for him, with a very accurate preliminary design. I've wanted to create a new style of little trimaran like this for a long time. So it was really a thrill to be given the unexpected opportunity to work on a project like this, which ended up as the *Sardine Run* trimaran.

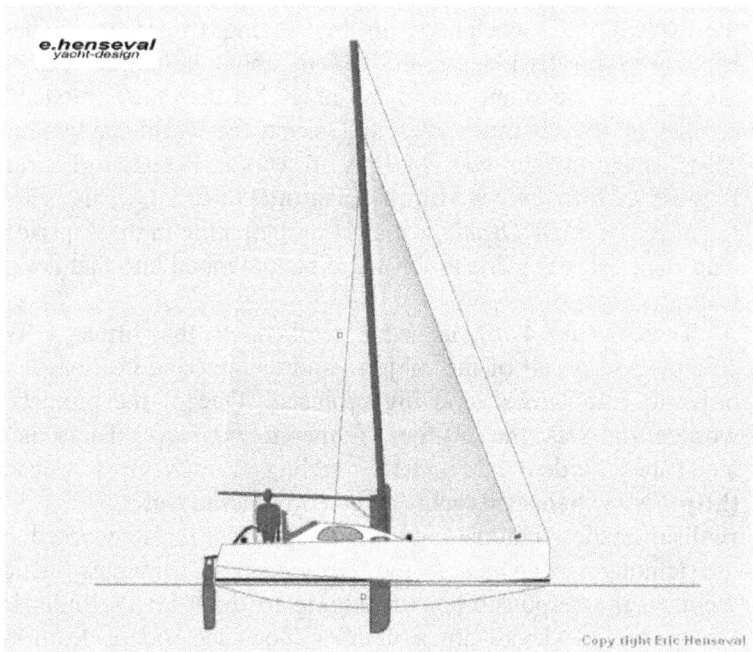

Sardine Run was created especially with homebuilders in mind. It is designed for construction in marine-grade plywood

An Interview with Eric Henseval

and epoxy. The construction method will be standard "*stitch and glue*." And its ama construction will be the same as the main hull.

Sardine Run's length overall is 5.50m (18 feet). When fully assembled its beam will be 4.45m (14 feet 7 inches wide). It will weigh a very light 300 kg (661.4 pounds).

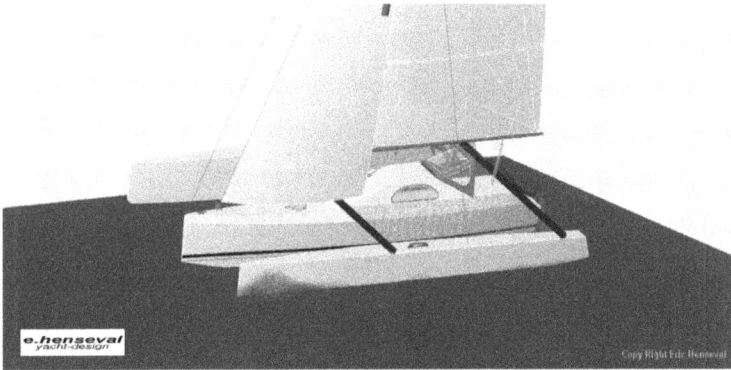

The boat will basically be assembled around 4 female bulkheads that are fixed on a horizontal frame. This frame forms a very simple "plug." Then the hull shell will be stitched and glued together around the bulkheads. This allows the boat to go together without stressing the hull form in any way. This same basic process is used to put together the amas.

I've estimated that it will take around 300 hours to construct the boat. This includes how long it should take for most homebuilders. The first Sardine Run prototype is being constructed at the time of this writing. It should be completed around March of 2010.

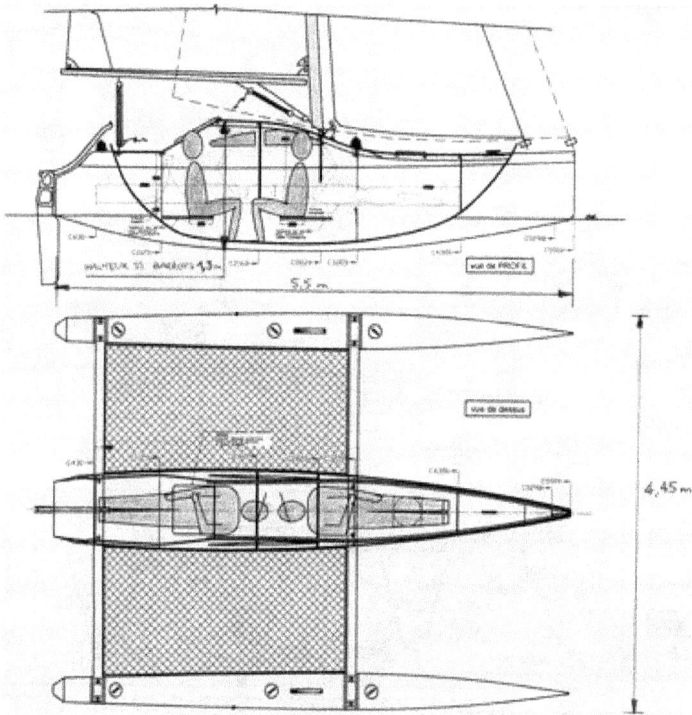

Sardine Run's crossbeams will be made out of aluminum. A builder will simply use 3mm tubes that are 100mm in diameter. The beams will attach to the main hull and floats with 10mm diameter bolts. I designed easy access to the bolt nuts through little inspection hatches in the hulls.

An Interview with Eric Henseval

This method permits the structure to be simple and strong, while avoiding any of the problems often caused by folding systems, including high cost. Using simple crossbeams in a boat this size makes economical sense. The simplicity also allows the boat to go together quickly. It should only take about 30 minutes to assemble or disassemble the boat.

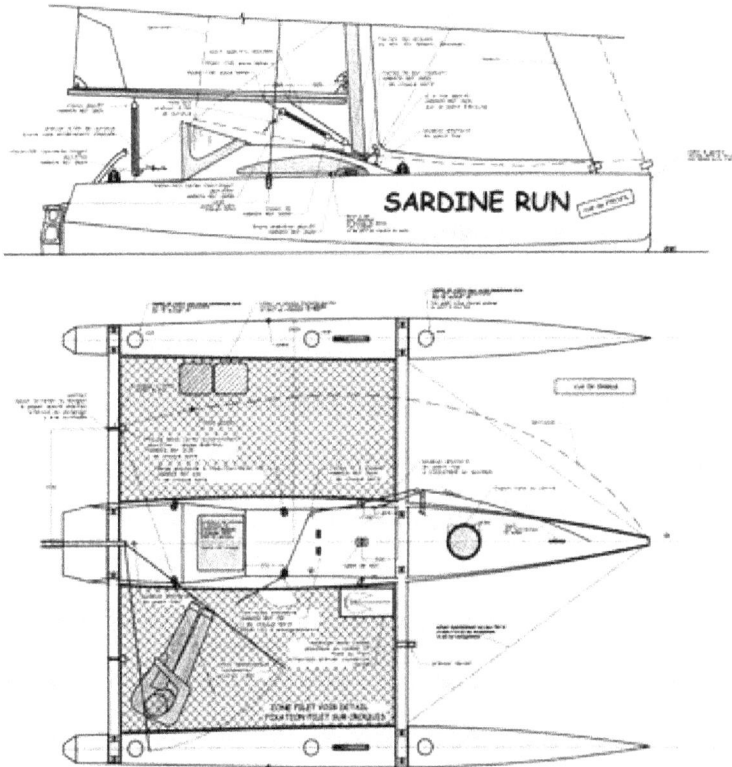

Sardine Run will certainly be trailerable. The amas can be brought side by side with the main hull while the boat is on the trailer. There will be 2 light "female plugs on rollers" (in plywood) to move each ama at the good beam. Then the amas will bolt onto the crossbeams. The boat will be entirely mounted while on the trailer. Then the sailboat can be put into the water.

The plans do not contain directions for a wooden mast. They call for a homebuilder to acquire a factory-made aluminum rig instead. All of the specifications and cotations will be provided. All a builder has to do is take them to a rig manufacturer of their choice and have the mast fabricated.

I've also created a very detailed sail plan for this boat. A homebuilder will be able to take them to any sailmaker and have sails made that specifically match this boat. For peak performance, I recommend the sloop rig. An asymetrical spinnaker can be used instead of a general gennaker, however, if the sailor prefers.

I think the time it takes to set up this sailing rig will be comparable to the time it takes to set up a Hobie 18 rig (or similar). This means the total time needed to mount everything is probably going to be about 45 minutes. It's entirely possible to use this boat for daysailing, but it may not be ideal if a sailor doesn't want to take the time required to mount and rig the boat each time they take it out on the water.

An Interview with Eric Henseval

The Sardine Run will ideally sail with just one or two sailors on board. Keeping the crew weight down is really important on a small boat like this in order to keep the performance level up.

The Sardine Run should offer comfortable sailing *for its size*. When compared to other trimarans in this range, the nets on this boat are going to be placed 70cm above the water. That is a very high position for them considering the length of the boat. The crossbeams will be sufficiently high above the waves and will also avoid any "braking" in them, while keeping sprays to a minimum. This will help keep the ride drier.

In addition to the small aft cockpit, sailors will be able to do much of the sailing while seated on floating cushions placed on the nets. That should also help make things more comfortable.

Sardine Run features a cabin for 2 persons. There is 1.30 m of headroom and 80 cm of width. Both individuals can be seated in front of each other at the center of the boat. And sailors can go inside the cabin even when the boat is sailing if they need to. It's also possible to fit a Porta-Potty inside.

If two sailors are going camp-cruising then there won't be room for a fixed cook stove or small refrigerator. But if a sailor is single-hand sailing then these items can fit into the area designed as the forward berth.

The first boat is due to be launched very soon. I will be able to speak more about its actual sailing performance in a few months. The Sardine Run is an atypical design. I think it will be able to reach 15 knots at times. This assumes a good sailor is handling the boat properly in the right weather conditions.

"Drawing Up Boats For Individuals"

Sardine Run is now available in both plan *and* kit form. (The kit is available in France and in Europe from Sardine boats)· The plans are very detailed and I've tried to make them easy to read.

The building plans include the sail plan and other specifications. There is a plan for the main hull forms, the float forms, the arrangement of sections, a deck plan (with all of the hardware detailed and listed), and general structure plans (including main hull, with detailed views of scantlings, hull structure, deck details, and all bulkheads), rudder form, centerboard structure, chainplates, plexiglass hatches, crossbeam assembly and materials list. There are also additional sketches of the centerboard, the spectra triangle under the forward crossbeam and details of the netting (with its assembly method).

An Interview with Eric Henseval

If a sailor likes Sardine Run but hasn't built a sailboat before then this trimaran would still be a suitable building project. From a construction perspective, I can describe this boat as a really big kayak with simple hull forms. This includes the floats as well as the central hull.

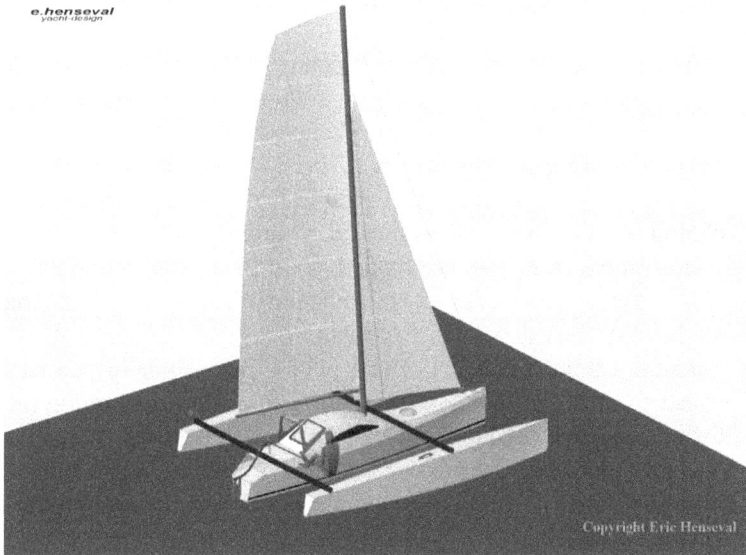

Sardine run is designed with big volumes in the amas and also features good freeboard for safety. She is calculated to have the floats above the water at rest, and to avoid drag, even in loading conditions. The full additional load can reach 270kg and higher in order to stay balanced.

All boats have their advantages and drawbacks. But I don't think there are lots of boats with crossbeams as high above the water as Sardine Run.

She is also designed in light of the French racing trimarans -- even if she isn't a pure racing boat. I wanted to draw upon my past work with the big racers and apply it to this boat by giving it the simplicity, the economy and the experience of modern racing hulls. It should also be an interesting sailboat to use for "camping" navigations.

If I were to compare Sardine Run with other small tris on the market I'd say it's a boat for just about everybody. I answer potential customer questions from individuals who are 18 to 50 years old. Sardine Run appeals to a wide range of people because it's reasonable.

The ideal customer could be a person who wants to sail fjords in Scotland, in good autonomy, for a whole week. Sardine Run's appearance may also be a selling benefit; she looks like a bigger racing boat, whereas, she is only 5.50m in length with 2 berths.

I try to create boats for every kind of person, while always keeping in mind both economy and simplicity. One of my goals for customers is to be able to feel good about their future boat. I'd like them to even feel "well married" to her ... and for that, they have to trust their own feelings.

I really think I can help most people have their own boat in respect to their wishes. For example, I'm currently working on a 50-foot racing monohull that can be sailed even by individuals who are physically disabled. I enjoy drawing up boats for individuals with a singular personality -- as long as the project is reasonably doable.

The most beautiful sailing experience I ever enjoyed with a multihull was on a boat delivery, where our crew sailed from La Trinité to La Rochelle (in France) during winter. It was a very fast navigation on a 40-foot catamaran with no cabin.

The boat was built using lots of carbon fiber, had a very low freeboard, a huge wing-mast and the rudders were positioned forward. The *average* speed reached was 18 knots and, on what turned out to be a very wet trip, we lost all our papers and money during the ride.

After delivering the boat, our crew had to sleep without any food in a railway-station with a few very sympathetic homeless people. We got to do that after enjoying a wonderful navigation on a marvelous multihull valued at several millions of dollars. If we had Sardine Run we could have slept inside its main hull instead! ☺

…………………………….

For more information about Henseval Yacht Design visit **http://www.hensevalyachtdesign.com/** & **http://hensevalyd-english.jimdo.com/** (the English version of his website). Contact information for Eric Henseval can be found on these websites.

Among the Multihulls
A Memoir by Jim Brown
Volumes 1 & 2

Multihull pioneer Jim Brown, after fifty years of designing, building and seafaring in catamarans, trimarans and proas, is publishing a personal memoir in 2 volumes. In these pages, he describes modern multihulls as, *"an entire new genus in the phylum of surface watercraft,"* and enthusiasts get to revel in the lore of these vessels with Jim's mesmerizing storytelling.

The focus of this two-volume work is on how the advent of modern multihulls has shaped the author's life and the lives of his colleagues, clients, shipmates and family. Volume 1 recounts multihull incidents and milestones from the 1940s to the 1970s. Volume 2 covers from the '70s to the present. Brown identifies the cultural and geopolitical context from which modern multihulls emerged; explains the phases of their design, construction and application; and traces their progress from derision to acceptance in yachting, ocean racing, seasteading, and in commercial and military service.

Largely autobiographical, the books contain many sea stories of the author's and his client's escapades, mishaps and achievements. Brown first relates the adventures of "seasteading" in foreign waters for years with his family. And then, in the second volume, he becomes a kind of Johnny Appleseed for multihull peasant watercraft in remote settings of the developing world. He concludes, at age 76, with his personal worldview; how it has been shaped by incidents in the books, and draws scenarios of what multihulls may mean to the future of humankind.

For more information visit
www.smalltrimarans.com/r/brown.html

Chapter 9

An Interview with
Ronan Quin-Huard

Builder of the
Bandit 800 Trimaran

Editor's Note: This chapter features a very short interview with Ronan Quin-Hard, who works as a builder and promoter of a French trimaran design called the Bandit 800. Ronan kindly participated in an interview with me even though our conversation was very limited due to the language barrier. I was able to piece together the following text, though, based upon our brief phone session and the information he sent me via email. Even though this chapter doesn't include nearly enough unique info about this sailboat, the Bandit 800 is a design I think readers will enjoy in this book.

I've sailed for about the last 15 years. When I was younger I took vacations next to the ocean and was drawn to sailing. After learning how to sail myself, I went on to teach others how to sail.

I really liked sailing multihulls. I was drawn to them because of their performance. In addition to speed, I think they also offer more comfortable sailing. There is a sensation I enjoy when sailing a multihull that a monohull just doesn't provide.

There came a point in my professional life that I started wanting a job related to sailing and boats. And I'd hoped to be able to work primarily with multihulls because of my personal preference for them. That led me into the work of building and promoting sailboats, especially multis, which I've done for the past 6 years.

In 2006, a man named Gerard Rumen formed the shipyard I now work for. Our yard builds the *Bandit 800* trimaran. Gerard obtained the building plans for this boat from Pierre Rolland, who is a well-known naval architect here in France. Pierre is the designer of this sailboat.

Pierre has a history of sailing and designing primarily racing sailboats. Although most of his sailboats in the past have been monohulls, he now includes multis in his portfolio. Our boat building business pays royalties to Pierre so we can use his patent and make these boats.

The Bandit 800 Trimaran

We built the first prototype for this boat in 2006. This included finishing the deck plan and layout of the ship.

This prototype was first presented at the Le Grand Pavois boat show in La Rochelle. Our first 2 orders for the boat were placed at that show. And we've been periodically fulfilling orders ever since. Our shipyard now has a new owner because Mr. Rumen sold his interest in 2008. But that doesn't interfere with our current production of the Bandit 800.

We've just completed plans for a second version of this sailboat because prospective buyers were increasingly asking for more finished accommodations inside the trimaran. This means we're now offering 2 versions of the Bandit. The first is our original "racer-cruiser" model. And the second one is our newer "cruiser" version, which offers a newer interior layout inside the cabin.

There are also a couple of other differences between these 2 versions, apart from the interior. These differences obviously create the type of boat an owner wants.

More Small Trimarans

The racer-cruiser version offers a carbon mast that is, of course, lighter than an aluminum mast. And it features 2 asymmetrical daggerboards that enable better performance. It's regarded as a bit less comfortable because its interior layout is simpler than the newer model. The racer-cruiser features a front cabin with only one bunk for sleeping in the back of it.

The newer cruiser model features a much bigger cabin with different portions. There is a front area, a small living-room with amenities in the center, and then a separate cabin-space in the back. We've worked hard to improve the interior layout of the boat for those who really want things to be even more comfortable and convenient.

The volume inside the cruiser cabin is fairly spacious. Six sailors can sleep inside quite comfortably. The front part of the cabin is large enough to accommodate 2 adults. The middle part of the cabin can sleep 2 persons. And 2 people can also sleep on padding at the back portion of this interior space.

The cruiser version also has an aluminum mast and a single pivoting daggerboard in the main hull.   This pivoting daggerboard gives the cruiser more stability and added safety. The boat can navigate in shallow water much more easily with the single daggerboard too.

There are many sailors who are attracted to the Bandit 800 trimaran.   But in general, we've found that prospective buyers want the boat for primarily three things: fast cruising (with accommodations), pure daysailing, and single-hand sailing.

Now that we're offering 2 versions of this boat, customers will be able to get more of the type of sailing they really want. Other trimarans on our market seem to be geared towards one or the other -- either racing *or* cruising.

Even though the Bandit 800 is 26-feet long, it can be taken further out into the ocean than a typical coastal cruiser.   The

Bandit performs quite well in bigger seas; it's able to navigate the higher waves very well. The large volume in the main hull also helps its overall performance in heavier weather conditions.

Sailors will stay pretty dry in waves up to about 1.5 meters high, which is pretty good for a small trimaran. But sailors will need to have their foul weather gear on in bigger waves. The cockpit area generally permits very comfortable sailing. And all of the control lines are available to those seated inside the cockpit.

The hulls for the Bandit 800 are made using a vacuum-molding technique. This method guarantees good laminate homogeneity and light weight for the entire structure. The material is made of sandwich PVC foam inserted between two laminate glass/polyester skins. Inside fittings attached to the hulls are made of PVC/glass/polyester materials, while some structural elements are strengthened with unidirectional carbon tissue.

Using these types of materials offers light construction, which can allow for increased performance. But they also provide rigidity and strength throughout the craft.

The sailboat utilizes a convenient folding system that is similar to well-known ones on the market. It takes about 2 minutes to fold the crossbeams so the floats can be brought alongside the main hull. This is a great asset when seeking out a smaller harbor site to dock the boat.

More Small Trimarans

Unfolding the trimaran allows its cockpit to be extended outward with two pivoting benches (you can see a picture at the **http://www.multido.fr** for a view of this). The handling of the boat is then increased, thanks to the angulation of the arms with the main hull by 12° (=dihedral angle), allowing navigation/sailing in heavy sea conditions and making it easier to stay dry.

This boat isn't really "trailerable" in the sense that a sailor is going to take it to different sailing venues all the time. It takes a lot of effort to get the boat onto a trailer because the amas are quite large. The folded beam width is 12 feet, which is obviously another challenge for road transport. And it can take as much as half a day to put this boat safely on a trailer in order to take it on the road.

An Interview with Ronan Quin-Huard

The Bandit 800's designer wanted to create the boat with increased volume in the floats because it's a huge benefit in terms of performance. The size of the amas is a very important aspect of the design. The compromise, however, was giving up easy trailerability.

We consider the Bandit 800 to be a modern high-performance sailboat. The racer version of this trimaran can potentially reach maximum speeds of nearly 20 knots. But common cruising speeds are easily in the range of 10-12 knots.

Small multihull enthusiasts seem to really like the Bandit's look. We get lots of compliments on its modern design. It has the appearance of a racer and many sailors really like that. It's very likely this may help preserve the boat's resale value too. Potential buyers are always interested in the eye-appeal of any boat they're considering for purchase.

We completely build each boat for our customers and try to take care of their individual needs. This includes making certain adaptations for each order to provide a more customized product. And if anything ever breaks or needs replacement then we can supply whatever parts are necessary.

We've found that those who are interested in the Bandit 800 are sailors who have lots of passion for high performance but also want a certain degree of comfort. This may include single-hand sailors or those who want to take family and friends along for an extended cruise. So we don't necessarily have just one certain type of customer.

One recent Bandit 800 purchaser is 69 years old and lives in Senegal, on the west coast of Africa. He has a reputation for being a sailor who really knows the ocean and how to sail it well. He has done lots of sailing with his family over the years.

It turns out that he bought a Bandit 800 trimaran because he wanted it to be part of his plan to offer "humanitarian vacations." What he wants to do is have individuals visit Senegal and do things such as dig wells and participate in other work projects in order to help people throughout the country. But part of these

More Small Trimarans

vacations will include fun sailing time out in the African ocean in the Bandit 800.

....

For more about the Bandit 800 Trimaran visit
http://www.multido.fr/eng/index.htm
Contact information for Chantier Naval MULTID'O is available on this website.

Chapter 10

An Interview with Steve Isaac
(a.k.a. "Chief"),
Founder of WaterTribe
&
Matt Layden
Designer of the
"Tridarka" Raider

Steve Isaac Interview

I've been interested in wilderness/watercraft type stuff since my childhood. I grew up in southern Minnesota and there was a lot of canoeing available in my area. One of the seminal moments in my younger years was reading Thor Heyerdahl's book, *Kon-Tiki*. That got me all fired up. I started building rafts and floating down the river and dreaming about boats. That's kind of where it all got started for me.

More Small Trimarans

After getting married, my wife and I lived in Minnesota. We both decided that if we wanted to get into sailing then we'd have to move to another part of the country because you can only go sailing for 3 months out of the year up in Minnesota. So we moved to Florida in 1979.

Our first sailboat was a 15-footer. We went on to enjoy several small sailboats over the years, including a 21-foot *Sea Pearl* and 26-foot *Islander*. The Islander was a beautiful, fast boat. I eventually got interested in kayaking also. It just seems like we've always had a small boat around.

I love the freedom sailing offers. And I like small boats in general because of their ability to let you feel very close to nature.

Going out for a day sail is enjoyable for me because getting out on the water is always fun. But that's not my first love. I primarily love going sailing for a few consecutive days ... with a destination in mind. I like going from point A to point B.

I'm often referred to as "*Chief*" nowadays because I founded a one-person company called *WaterTribe*. Back in the year 2000 I read some books by the guys who call themselves the "Tsunami Rangers." Their books described what these guys saw as different "tribes" within water sports. They referred to various groups of people having similar interests within the various areas of water sports and they gave them names like: the Surftribe, the Downriver Whitewater Tribe, the Canoetribe, etc.

That got me thinking about those names. One day, the name WaterTribe popped into my head. I passed this new word by one of my buddies and he thought it was pretty cool.

The whole purpose of WaterTribe is giving sailors an excuse to get out on the water together for a few days each year here in Florida. It started out being an online magazine, which it kind of still is. But late in 2000 I got the idea for doing a race I referred to as the *Everglades Challenge*. This race is really what the name WaterTribe is associated with now.

The race begins at Tampa Bay and goes down to Key Largo.

It's about 300 miles long - give or take a few - depending upon which course a sailor chooses to follow. This event is open to watercraft that includes kayaks and small sailboats. Participating boats are divided into 6 classes, which are all described on WaterTribe's website.

The purpose of the Everglades Challenge Race is to sort of cram everything a sailor would have to do if they were on a long expedition into a time frame of about a week. Many boaters will never be able to get away for months at a time in order to go on a long expedition. But most sailors can get away for a week. So that's what this race is all about.

WaterTribe appeals to people that like to go camp-cruising. But they also like to have it be somewhat challenging, with a little bit of adventure sprinkled in. There are a few racers mixed in with our group, but basically, it's composed of people who love to be out on the water in their small boats.

"The Tridarka Raider"

I really wanted a boat that would be especially suited to compete in an event such as the Everglades Challenge. This led me to start a building project that ended up as a trimaran design I call the *"Tridarka Raider."*

The word Tridarka was inspired by George Dyson's book *Baidarka*. On page 122 of my version, from the 1988 printing, there is a picture showing a trimaran version of a Biadarka taken to the extreme. It inspired me to name my new sailboat "Tridarka" since it was a tri. The "Raider" part of the name was inspired by the various RAID type races and my Viking heritage.

I've had the idea for this unique boat in my head for years. I even built 6-foot models of it before actually building the prototype. I used hull design software to come up with a hull shape but eventually got Matt Layden to design the Tridarka Raider for me.

A side goal was to make the Tridarka a boat others could

build. I thought it would be neat if, one year during the Everglades Challenge, there were 6 Tridarka Raiders at the starting point getting ready to race against each other. That's another reason why I got Matt involved. I knew I could build a boat. But Matt is an infinitely better designer than me and he could also produce professional plans for anyone else who wanted to build a Tridarka. I asked Matt if he'd help me take my ideas for this boat and turn them into a real boat with real plans. Thankfully, he said, "*Yes.*"

In designing this boat, I wanted to place more emphasis on cruising capabilities than on its ability to race. I do like going fast when I'm cruising in order to cover more ground, but I really wanted a boat that was very seaworthy.

The Tridarka did turn out to be a fast boat, although there are certainly small trimarans out there that are faster. But it's really designed to be a comfortable, adventure-racing sailboat for WaterTribe type of events.

"Self-Bailing Capability"

Matt came up with a great finished design. He and I discussed the specifications and then he formulated it for me so I could build it. I haven't found a single mistake in the design in relation to what I wanted for this boat. It was fun to build and it's fun to sail.

I don't look at the Tridarka as "better" than other boats; I just think it's "different." There are other small trimarans out there but I haven't seen many with the features of the Tridarka. It's really in a class by itself.

Even though the Tridarka Raider is a trimaran, I took things from other kinds of boats that I'm familiar with in order to incorporate them within it. For example, I wanted a boat that would sail like a sailboat and not a kayak. Yet I wanted a cockpit in the Tridarka that feels like a comfortable kayak.

I wanted the cockpit to be fairly open and large ... but not too large. I also desired the cockpit to be above the waterline so the boat could be self-bailing. The way it turned out, the Tridarka can take green water over its bow and it probably won't come into the cockpit. But if it does, the water will just run out of the boat because of its self-bailing capability.

The length of the Tridarka measures a little less than 21 feet. The hulls can just be made with ¼ inch plywood, with one layer of fiberglass and epoxy on the inside and one layer on the outside. My prototype, however, had Kevlar, carbon fiber and fiberglass on the bottom of it, which made it very tough. The boat could bounce right off a submerged drum in the water and not skip a beat.

I put a lot of money into the prototype in order to try different things out. But other builders will be able to build a Tridarka much more cost-effectively than what I built mine for. It took me about 8 months to get the bulk of it built. Then I spent another couple of months doing little things here and there. I don't think building the Tridarka took very long when considering that building a trimaran is like building 3 boats, except the connecting structure holds the 3 separate hulls together.

A homebuilder can build the Tridarka from either plans or full-length patterns. It may even be offered as a kit one day. A kit would be priced more than just the plans because it would offer precision cuttings and those are expensive to have created. Acquiring such precision cut parts, though, would save builders time.

If a homebuilder has time, then building from plans will probably be more cost effective. My current blog goes over the building process in quite a bit of detail. There are lots of photos available too. I'm going to provide some kind of format to offer builders this building information for the Tridarka even if it's not featured on my blog in the future.

"A Perfect Boat For Surfing"

Seaworthiness was the main criteria for this sailboat. This boat really handles a bigger sea really well. And there is just enough rocker and floatation in the hulls to enable it to effectively catch waves.

When you're surfing fast, the bow on the boat doesn't bury at all. It has enough lift in the bow and enough curve there to make it a perfect boat for surfing. Feeling the acceleration when you're surfing waves in the Tridarka is pretty thrilling. I'm able to feel the acceleration of waves underneath me even when they're under a foot tall.

The hulls of the Tridarka are so skinny that it doesn't take much to push them. There is practically no resistance against these hulls. And when running downwind on a broad reach my experience is that the sails designed for this boat work well.

The boat handles just like I wanted it to. And it's pretty fast, even though speed wasn't the main criteria. The boat coasts along nicely in fairly light winds. I've passed boats in the Tridarka that have twice its sail area in light breezes.

Matt Layden Interview

My dad's family was originally from Connecticut and then moved to Long Island. I got into sailing because my father was a boatman, and my grandfather before him. As early as I can recall, boats have always been a part of our family.

My dad bought an old 27-foot wooden cruiser that was falling apart and rebuilt it when I was about 3 or 4 years old. So I've been sailing since I was a kid.

I grew up drawing models and then real boats. There were always boat ideas in my mind. An interest in boat design was always a part of me and I just sort of grew into this sort of work. My dad also had some training in marine design back in college. He imparted some of that knowledge to me over the years.

After high school I had some time to begin making my own boats and go cruising. I got to experiment with different ideas and try things out in order to find out what worked and what didn't.

My boat designs have often focused on small cruisers because that's what interests me. I've designed and built about half a dozen of my own and have designed a few others for clients. But I've also designed kayaks, rowboats and various other types of small boats.

"Modern Small Trimaran Design"

I first met Steve Isaac during a WaterTribe event. We sat down together at the finish line after an Everglades Challenge Race and he talked to me about his ideas for a new sailboat. Steve said he wanted to build a small, lightweight, expedition and cruising type of trimaran.

Steve shared many of his ideas with me because he knew I had a professional background in boating. Our first meeting was very informal. I didn't think it would turn into a design contract. It was just 2 guys sharing what we thought were practical and workable plans for this new boat idea in Steve's mind. From that point though, I started thinking about his boat too.

A couple years later Steve came and seriously asked me if I thought the concepts he'd shared with me earlier were workable. I really thought the boat Steve wanted to build was worthwhile. Steve had already collected tons of ideas from other small boat enthusiasts and had spoken to a couple of other designers about this project. From that point things just took off.

Steve and I both sort of initially worked out plans for this new tri he called the "Tridarka Raider" over a period of about a year. The boat grew (on paper) a little bigger and a bit heavier as time went on.

The Tridarka started out as a simple, lightweight double outrigger canoe, like you see pictures of from the Pacific Islands. But those boats don't really offer much hull volume or displacement. As our concept grew, we massaged the Tridarka to be more powerful and safer. So it gradually became a full buoyancy, modern small trimaran design.

"Safe At Sea"

The Tridarka's features were sort of driven by Steve's wish

list for the boat. He wanted a boat that would be safe to be out in all kinds of weather. He really wanted the boat to be able to surf downwind too … that was a big goal. Steve really wanted to be able to surf safely in a big storm of wind and sea.

Steve also wanted some other distinctive features. For example, he wanted some overhang that formed a sort of whaleboat-looking bow, as opposed to a vertical bow with a full length of waterline. We tried to work little ideas like this into the prototype.

The Tridarka is designed to be very buoyant. There's a lot of lift in the bow and lots of rocker, sheer and dynamic lift throughout. This means the boat can be sailed in 15-20 knots of wind down a breaking wave and not bury her bows in the water. The boat won't stop and get broached by the sea.

The Tridarka is a little lower in sail area than some other small trimarans out there of similar size because it's meant to be more of an expedition type of boat than a day racer. But its displacement-to-length and power-to-weight ratios are fairly standard.

I'm sure the Tridarka can comfortably carry a good bit more sail than what its standard plans call for. After we increased the volume of the floats I'd say its sail area could probably be increased safely by about 50%. That would make it a higher performance day racer if the priority was to go faster instead of being safer for long expedition cruising.

Steve's goal of being safe at sea was more important than simply going fast. The Tridarka's buoyancy and lifty bows factor prominently in this, but the cockpit is also self-bailing if waves do enter into the boat. The cockpit is an open area between 2 bulkheads that sits *above* the waterline.

The boat was originally designed to be quite light. The prototype got heavier though because Steve wasn't always able to find the lighter materials we were looking for. The weight of certain parts doubled because the carbon fiber Steve wanted for some things wasn't available on the market at the time. So Steve's Tridarka Raider ended up being very strong and a bit heavier than it was originally supposed to be.

The heavier prototype didn't turn out to be bad though. The sailboat is seriously strong. I'm sure it could handle accidents and rough weather a lot better than most production boats her size.

The Tridarka's plans currently offer the original wooden mast rig and beam system for connecting the floats. It could take a sailor a bit of time to get the boat set up to go sailing if they go this route. There are 4 half-akas, or crossbeams, that fit into the main hull and also attach the floats. Everything is lashed together ... 16 lashings in all ... in order to hold the boat together.

The initial design calls for the crossbeams to be constructed with box sections of wood. They're relatively simple for a homebuilder to construct. They can be made on one jig with a single strong back. This jig would serve to make all 4 half-beams. A builder would just lay out shaped blocks against the strong back and then lay down 4 pre-shaped pieces of wood in the right order and glue everything together.

After using the above system for a while, Steve ended up changing the akas on his prototype to help it be more easily trailered and then set up to go sailing. He had an aluminum fabricating company design the beams in order to create a sliding system that is much faster than taking things completely apart for trailering. Steve's prototype then didn't have to be put back together again to get the boat set up to go out on the water. His boat can probably be ready to go from the trailer into the water for sailing in about half an hour.

We plan on developing drawings for the sliding beam system Steve had made for his prototype so customers can get their own aluminum beams fabricated. This will allow their boat to be setup a lot quicker once it's off the trailer to go sailing. It'll allow the amas to be either pulled out or pushed back in towards the main hull by just removing a couple of pins.

The main hull and amas are basically just straightforward stitch and glue wood construction. The wood pieces can be cut to spec and then stitched together on very simple, temporary frames. This frame isn't a full mold; it's just a set of forms tacked to a temporary strong back. That allows the hull panels to be wired up and glued together with epoxy to keep their shape and hold the centerline straight. The amas are also built using basic plywood/stitch and glue construction. They're pretty much just fully decked-over single chine plywood hulls.

Plans for the Tridarka may eventually come with paper patterns that can be used to cut the various plywood sections for building the boat. That would make things even easier for homebuilders because they wouldn't have to measure the plywood pieces before cutting them.

The Tridarka hulls can be made with 4-millimeter marine ply and sheathed inside and out with 6-10 ounces of fiberglass cloth and epoxy resin. Steve really went way beyond that for his prototype, though, because he wanted a boat that would be super strong. He built the hulls using 4-mil ply and then covered them with 5 ounces of carbon fiber followed by 5 ounces of Kevlar and then 4 ounces of fiberglass. His model was heavily reinforced.

I'm guessing that a builder could build this boat in 10 months to a year, if they steadily worked on it part time. If somebody was familiar with stitch and glue boat building and had 40-60 hours a week to work on this boat then it could probably be built in about 3-4 months.

"A Single Bat-wing Cat Sail"

Steve and I went back and forth over half a dozen ideas when it came to the rig. We thought hard about a used sloop rig borrowed from an existing sailing dinghy. But Steve wanted something a little more distinctive. The rig that ended up on the Tridarka is actually very suited to the boat, which is a single bat-wing cat sail on a carbon fiber mast.

Being one-of-a-kind, all of the parts have to be custom-made, so it's more expensive than a conventional rig. It's a little bit stiffer than your usual cat-sail type of rig too. The custom Tridarka rig is sort of a cross between a sliding gunter and a gaff sail, in which the upper couple of feet of the sail protrudes above the mast on a sliding yard. So the mast can be a little bit shorter and the whole rig can be a little bit lighter overall.

I'd done a couple of bat-wing sails before and liked them a lot. They're a little bit "busy" when it comes to parts and things. There are lots of small parts with a rig like this but it enables fast sailing. It's a bit lighter than a traditional Bermuda type of sail for its given amount of sail area. And because it's fully battened it's sort of like a Hobie cat sail in that it forms a fairly rigid wing that doesn't flap or fly around or try to shake itself to pieces when tacking.

There's nothing really new about the Tridarka sail. It's a compilation of various older technologies that have been around for over 120 years. But we were able to pull them together in order to form a unique rig that really works well for this boat. I actually think this sail is easier to work with than a traditional sloop rig.

Steve used a company called Forte (**www.fortecarbon.com/mar_battens.html**) to make his mast on their equipment. They were able to make the mast size he needed but it was a little pricey.

Homebuilders can always make their own wooden mast. Mast plans can be included in with the stock boat plans if they want it. The plans already include specs for a tapered aluminum flagpole mast. So there are several ways a sailor who builds a Tridarka can go and a number of resources are available.

Any sail maker who has experience making multihull sails will be able to make the Tridarka's bat-wing sail. There shouldn't be a big issue there at all. We've included notes in the plans written for sail makers that should answer any questions one might have. But all the dimensional info needed is basically in the drawings.

If somebody wants to put more sail area on a Tridarka then I'd probably say that an off-the-shelf sloop rig would be the way to go. A sailor could also purchase a used rig from one of the racing classes, such as a Lightning, 470 class sailing dinghy or 505 performance sailboat ... something in the 16-18 foot class size. That's often an inexpensive way to get a fully functioning rig.

"Ideal For Camp-Cruising"

The Tridarka Raider is a fairly comfortable boat to sail. There never seems to be a need to hike out onto the amas to balance the boat. Steve never put a hiking stick onto the tiller, although a sailor could do that if they wanted to.

The one thing lacking on the seating designed for this boat is a comfortable back. There is fairly comfortable seating on the level of the akas, with your feet down in the cockpit well. But there is no backrest to lean against. I'd recommend a sailor using one of those folding canvas seat backs that have been designed for bleacher-type stadium seats to create a nice back for sitting. I think such a canvas back would work well if applied to the seating on this boat. Some sit-on-top kayaks use a similar configuration for their seats.

I've sailed in the Tridarka and it was pretty dry up to about 20 knots of wind and 3 foot of sea. At that point some spray started coming over into the boat, which would hold true for just about any open boat this size. I thought the Tridarka was a good steady sailboat in those waves. Steve and I got a little wet, but we didn't get drenched.

The boat isn't really meant for more than 2 sailors. But if the dodger weren't set up then 4 people would easily fit inside the cockpit.

This boat is ideal for camp-cruising. You could put a tent out on the trampolines if you wanted. What I imagined for this boat was a custom tent that covered the entire cockpit, from seat edge to seat edge. It would allow 2 people to sleep on the cockpit seats and leave the footwell open for either moving around or storing gear. There's also a good deal of storage under the cockpit area, as well as in the watertight end compartments.

The Tridarka Raider was designed to be a light expedition boat, as opposed to either a day boat or cruising boat. It's really meant to be a sailboat that serves in between those 2 kinds of watercraft. Steve wanted to be able to use this boat to get out to the Dry Tortugas, which is a group of islands 70 miles out from the nearest populated land in Florida's Keys. So the Tridarka would be ideal for somebody who has a real desire to do lots of camp-cruising along the seacoast or inland waterways.

There are lots of interesting coastal places that can be reached by using the Tridarka. Although the Tridarka really isn't meant to go out to sea, the boat was made to be able to go offshore for an overnight passage during a good weather window. In other words, it can make overnight coastal passages in good weather conditions. These are the types of passages many sailors enjoy around Florida and other places.

One day, Steve and I sailed his Tridarka off Cedar Key, Florida. The wind was blowing 20-24 knots in the Gulf. And once we got outside the ship channel we encountered 5-6 foot waves. We tried out many different maneuvers in the boat and it felt very solid and steady, and handled great. We even surfed some waves that day and just had a great time.

....

For more information about the *Tridarka Raider* visit
http://www.WaterTribe.com/TridarkaRaider/
Plans for the *Tridarka* are available from Platypus Boats at
http://www.platypusboats.com/home.html

Designer Matt Layden may be contacted via email at
mattlayden@juno.com

Chapter 11

An Interview with
Paolo Bisol

Owner, Paolo Bisol Yacht Design
Designer, Tritium 720 Trimaran

When I was a boy growing up my family lived in a big city away from the coast. My parents were originally from the mountains and we always used to take vacations in the Alps. But about the time I was around 20, I decided it would be nice to see more of the sea. The sea had become very interesting to me.

I took one sailing course and then things sort of took off from there. I took a few more sailing courses afterwards and then found myself trying to take as many holidays as possible on the water. This has enabled me to enjoy sailing in different countries like Italy, England and France.

I'm more of a cruising sailor. Racing was never really something that personally interested me, even though I do race every now and then. When I have a chance, I try to take a long distance sailing trip. I completed a trans-Atlantic crossing once (from Gibraltar to Antigua, Caribbean) and on another occasion I crewed on a delivery from Germany to the Canary Islands. That is the kind of sailing I really enjoy. Whenever I get the opportunity to go out sailing I like the experience to be as long as possible.

Boat design work came as the result of a change in the professional area of my life. I used to be a designer of mostly mechanical type products. I'd started out in the aerospace industry. The company I worked for at the time made helicopters.

When I got into sailing I thought about matching my design skills with my passion for sailing. After moving to England in 1996 I took advantage of an opportunity to attend a university that offered a degree in marine design. I completed those courses about 10 years ago and I've been involved in the yacht design industry ever since.

"A Modern Design ...
While Keeping Things Simple"

There was a design competition in 2002 that was sponsored by Norsk Flerskrog Seilklubb, which is a Norwegian Multihull Club. They were looking for designs that would bridge the gap between small, sporty beach catamarans and bigger cruising multihull sailboats. They felt youngsters might tend to leave multihull sailing behind after getting older ... when they didn't want to experience the wet rides of beach cats anymore.

In the opinion of this multihull association, there wasn't much available in the area between beach cats and larger, more expensive catamarans. So they came up with the idea for a design competition.

I was working for a marine design business here in Cannes, France at that time and happened to discover the design competition on the Internet. After reading the criteria for the challenge I decided to enter it. That's how my small trimaran,

160

now referred to as the *Tritium 720*, was created. The Tritium won the competition that year.

Tritium 720

The brief I submitted to the committee had stay within the boundaries of a cost limitation and also had to feature a construction method that would allow the boat to be built by a typical homebuilder. This is a big reason why some of the Tritium's features are the way they are. I wanted to create a modern design while also keeping things as uncomplicated as possible.

Keeping things simple was very important. For example, I avoided designing a folding system for the boat. The crossbeams on this sailboat are much like a beach cat. The side floats bolt to the beams and then the beams slide into a socket within the central hull. The beams are then bolted in to secure their connection so they don't slide back out. The area between the beam and socket is a part of the central hull that bears the load for the connective system.

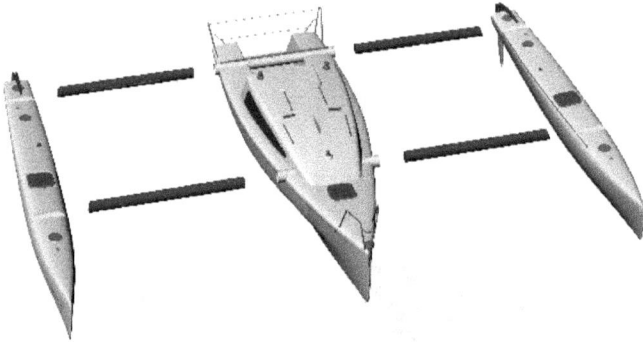

A homebuilder should be able to build the crossbeams on this boat without any problem. It's not hard; the process is fairly straightforward really. Each crossbeam is simply a tube. I sized these tubes so a homebuilder can actually buy commercial PVC piping and then laminate on top of it. So that will enable a builder to have a mold form that is commercially available anywhere.

The Tritium is demountable. But I don't think it's the sort of operation an owner/sailor is going to want to do every time they go sailing. So I wouldn't really say the boat is ideally "trailerable." Taking the boat apart would ideally be done after bringing the boat out of the water in order to prepare for storing at the end of a sailing season.

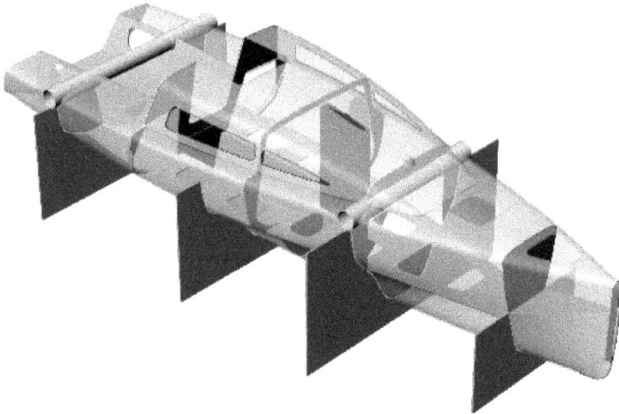

There are other designs out there that make for better trailerable boats even though taking the Tritium 720 apart isn't that big of a deal. Demounting is just a matter of removing a few bolts. But then you have to un-tension the trampolines and undo the rig and all of that. So that's why I don't see this being done regularly for daysailing.

The boat's hulls are constructed in a lightweight sandwich of PVC foam core and GRP skins. My plans don't go into detail about how to work with these composite materials but there are plenty of books available that describe the whole process involved with building a boat like this.

Using PVC foam core and GRP skin for the hull construction seemed very reasonable to me, especially since other established designers, including Ian Farrier, call for their boats to be made with these same composites.

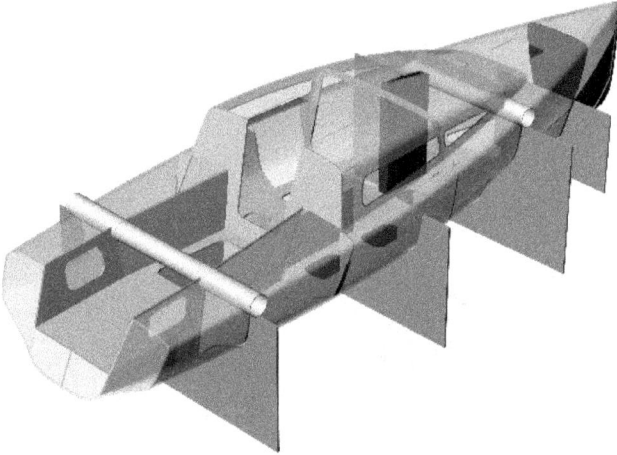

There are many blogs featuring homebuilders using composite materials to build their boats. It's not hard for many people who are serious about building a boat like this to get an understanding that it's doable.

People have asked me about building a plywood boat. And it's certainly understandable why they think building a boat with plywood might be a little easier to do. But one reason why I chose to design this boat to be built using composite materials is because there is compound curvature throughout the whole boat. You just couldn't build this boat in plywood.

I would encourage anyone who wants to build a boat (such as the Tritium 720) in composite materials to start out by building a little dinghy first. You'd want to do that before building a 7-meter trimaran like this in composite materials. Building a dinghy would help the builder get some experience using composites. Apart from that it shouldn't be a big deal.

"A Sporty Little Boat"

The Tritium 720 is designed to be a sporty little boat. I expect it to be fast. I also designed it so that the main hull would be very stable in fast conditions. That's why I put its 2 rudders on the side floats.

Paolo Bisol YACHT DESIGN ———— TRITIUM 720

This boat is ideal for 1 to 4 sailors. It would be a good fit for a small family too. The thing to keep in mind is that this craft is a daysailer and weekender type of boat. It's not a boat that should be used to venture far out offshore.

More Small Trimarans

It would be a good boat for camp-cruising. I'd say that up to 4 persons would be comfortable in the boat for camping purposes. There are 2 settees inside the cabin and a V-berth forward. Things like this all depend upon the final arrangement of the interior of the boat. Since the Tritium has been designed with self-builders in mind, the cabin layout is open enough to include a moveable sink, small stove and porta-potty, if a builder wants to install them.

Paolo Bisol YACHT DESIGN   TRITIUM 720

In terms of sail-to-weight ratio the Tritium 720 is probably close to a Corsair F-24. The sail area overall isn't that much different from what other boats its size normally feature.

I didn't want this boat to be "extreme." I was simply looking to create a sporty, well-performing boat. And I wanted it to be able to be used for family cruising if a sailor primarily wanted it for that purpose.

The main hull should not come out of the water unless a sailor is really pushing the boat hard. If it does, however, the two rudders on the side floats means the boat will still be fully controllable. That is a safety feature I felt should be added for a boat this size.

To get the mast and sail for this boat, a builder should have the rig I designed for it fabricated by suppliers who specialize in these things. They should go to a mast maker and get the mast specifically called for in my drawings.

I sometimes see trimarans out there that are comparable in size to the Tritium 720 and they advertise that beach cat rigs can be used on their boats. I don't quite understand that. When I did the calculations for my rig, I knew that a boat like this has a large "righting moment." This is important to note when taking into account the compression that has to go into the mast.

There is no way a little tube like one on a beach cat would be able to stand the loads required for this boat. So when I look at the calculations, I find that I've ended up with a mast section that would be scary to try and substitute with a beach cat rig.

If I were to put a Hobie Cat mast on this boat, then I don't know the limitations that I should have figured into things so the mast doesn't get overloaded. When I see beach cat rigs put on a trimaran this size I really think it's strange. I don't understand why those masts wouldn't just break if used on a regular basis.

I understand if a designer is trying to design a boat in such a way that will keep expenses down for builders. But are they telling those who build their boat that the beach cat sails should be reefed as soon as the wind strength increases? Beach cat rigs will never be able to bear the sort of righting moment that can develop on a 7-meter trimaran like this.

Multihull rigs are typically beefier than ones you'd see on a comparably sized monohull. You need bigger cables in the stays and shrouds and you need a pretty strong mast section if you want the mast to be able to bear the full compression required for the multihull. But sometimes I see others using beach cat rigs on a trimaran this size and I just don't get it.

"They Want To Go Fast"

The ride on this boat should be fairly dry and comfortable if you're in fair weather conditions. There are many boats around this size. I honestly can't tell whether the hull shape on this boat is going to be any drier or wetter than another boat. I think it would compare well with a Corsair or Dragonfly or any other similar sized boat that offers a modern hull shape. The main hull has the typical "tulip" section to deflect waves, and the side floats have relatively high freeboard. But these boats can go fast, and there will be spray around for sure.

The Tritium's floats are bigger than some other comparable trimarans out there. They're a thoroughly modern shape in terms of volume distribution too. I went with around a 200% volume distribution on these floats because I think that is ideal for a boat like this. I won't say this is always the "best" way to approach the issue. But right now, I feel it's the best solution for a small trimaran such as this.

The Tritium 720 is unique from other tris its size in that it's designed to be built with modern materials while also keeping things as simple as possible. I really like the way it turned out. It's good looking and modern and is designed with simplicity for a homebuilder to be able to build it using composite materials.

Sailors will go for a trimaran such as this because they want to go fast. No question about it. But if you have a catamaran this size then you won't have a boat that offers any accommodations. So a trimaran offers the higher performance of a relatively light multihull while giving sailors a boat they can use to go away for weekends because everyone can sleep inside the boat.

A trimaran like this can provide many enjoyable days of sailing at 15 knots. A monohull this size typically doesn't offer that kind of performance, especially if it features cruising accommodations. Trimarans are generally regarded to offer more deck area than monohulls. And most multihull sailors also see the fact that these sailboats heel less as an advantage.

Once in awhile, people ask me if this is the kind of a boat they can take offshore. I always tell them that any 7-meter sailboat, including a trimaran, should be strictly used along coastal areas. This is a nice boat. But nobody should attempt to challenge rough seas in it. A sailor must always be aware of the conditions in which they're sailing. I find myself having to remind people sometimes that a sports boat isn't made to cross an ocean.

If a sailor were thinking about building a boat like the Tritium 720 I'd encourage them to build something smaller first. Try building a hull using composite materials and see how things work out. It's always better to test yourself with an easy project than to get into a project that is over one's head.

If you think about it, there is a lot to build when constructing a trimaran. There are three hulls instead of just one. It can be more work than a monohull just because of that one aspect. So try building a dinghy first and see how it goes.

....

For more about the Tritium 720 Trimaran visit
http://www.paolobisol.com/home_en.htm
Contact information for Paolo Bisol can be found at this website.

Chapter 12

An Interview with Ted & Zac Warren

Proprietors of Warren Light Craft & Designers of the "Little Wing" Trimaran

We've both sailed dinghies from the time we were kids. One of the things about little boats that we love is that they can be so responsive. There is always a thrill when you sheet in a little boat and it takes off. Just the simplicity of it and feeling that you're going fast is a different feeling than when you're in a big boat.

This is one reason why our Little Wing Trimaran design appeals to so many individuals. It's really a new type of kayak that converts into a very fast sailboat for personal enjoyment.

We'd been playing around with some different design ideas and thought about designing a sit-on-top paddle-sailer with super-skinny hulls. So this boat is really what you might call a "two-for-one."

This is really the 3rd generation of kayak we've developed. One of the things we realized by looking at hydrostatics and trying to make boats go faster is that you have to reduce wetted surface area. With a pure kayak, the energy to move the boat has to come from the paddler, which isn't very much. In cruising mode, a typical paddler can only generate between 2 and 3 pounds of average force to drive the boat. So you have to design a kayak to be extremely efficient.

We were working on a paddle kayak that was 15.5 feet long and realized that it might serve as a perfect size for a sailing kayak. It just made sense to take what we'd learned from our sailboats and apply it to something that could become a boat that is *both* a competent kayak and a competent trimaran.

What we essentially did was take a hull that we'd developed over a period of 8 years, which was extremely efficient, and turn it into a sailboat. This meant that even just a little bit of wind was going to drive the boat. When you take the amas, akas, mast and sails off, you've got a terrific stand-alone kayak. But this high-performance kayak is also a high-end performance sailboat.

The Little Wing can even be *paddle-sailed* when the wind is extremely light and still be able to hit about 6 knots of boat speed with very little paddling effort. We were very aware of the ergonomics required for paddling and put as much space between the beams as we could in order to get enough clearance for a paddler to be able to paddle without any interference from them.

"Takes About 5-10 Minutes To Set Up"

The Little Wing isn't just trailerable ... it's cartopable. As a matter of fact, transporting the boat on top of a vehicle is actually our preferred method of taking it to the water. We've had one customer actually fit 2 of these boats on top of his *Scion xB*, which is a mid-size vehicle. He attached a set of racks with extra long bars and completely fit two Little Wing trimarans on it.

The Little Wing only takes about 5-10 minutes to set up for sailing after you take it off your car or trailer. We provide an assembly manual that shows customers how to do this, but the process is very simple. There are 8 pins that quickly fit the kayak hull together with the beams and outriggers. Then you pull the jib out (the jib also serves as the forestay) and pull the sail back. Then you clip the jib onto the top of the mast with carabiners, which we use with fast-pins on this model wherever possible. The mast step is a "pin and disc," which slides into the mast foot. Then you pull the mast up. (The mast only weighs 8 pounds).

Since the rigging always stays pretty much attached to the back beam of the boat you don't have to "re-rig" the boat every time you want to take it out sailing. You just basically have to pull the lines in place and you're ready to go.

There are 5 rigging lines in total. They sit right in front of the sailor, in what we refer to as the "command console" of the boat, in front of the cockpit's opening. The rudder is controlled with your feet (a common feature in kayaks) so your hands are always free to either handle the lines or paddle.

When the boat is in "full kayak mode" there are no sails on it at all. If most people saw the boat in full kayak mode they probably wouldn't know it was also a sailboat. The rigging comes off, the command console comes off and the brackets that hold the beams to the main hull come off. We tried to put a lot of thought into this so that if somebody wants to use the boat purely as a kayak at times then they can easily do so.

The boat is readily cartopable because everything is very light. The mast is super light and the kayak itself weighs just 28 pounds. Each ama only weighs about 8 pounds. This means virtually anyone can handle these parts by themselves.

An Interview with Ted & Zac Warren

The main hull and amas are made with a carbon-fiber foam core symmetrical sandwich construction. Carbon fiber is used on both sides of a high quality marine foam core product called *Core Cell*. This is how we kept the weight down. All of the really good production sailboats nowadays are using the Core Cell product.

Using carbon fiber with Core Cell also gives the boat a high degree of durability. If you have an impact against Core Cell it will dent but not delaminate. These hulls won't rot or absorb water either. They feature ideal properties for use in a marine environment.

Every boat is built to order. This allows us to offer lots of custom options with each boat. For example, some of our customers want their boat set up with "fishing options." Kayak fishing has taken off recently. So if a customer wants to use their Little Wing to go fishing then we can set up the boat with rod holders, plus other holders that make the boat easy to use when fishing.

We've even customized boats for things such as photography and environmental water sampling. The individual using the Little Wing for water monitoring had us fabricate custom holders that would contain his instruments and sampling equipment. We're setting up a boat now so the owner will be able to launch his boat from underneath a bridge. He'll be able to use some custom blocks to raise the mast while seated inside the cockpit out on the water.

We make the hulls here at our shop in Salem, Massachusetts. This means if somebody ever damaged his or her boat we'd be able to fix it ourselves. We can even make a hull that has been severely damaged by rocks look brand new.

We can fabricate a boat in just about any color a customer wants too. We offer 3 standard colors for the Little Wing trimarans that are included in the basic price: red, yellow pearl and white gold. But for a small additional fee we can create a boat in any custom color. We use very high-end automotive paint to color these boats. So we can match any car color, create metallic colors or even create "trick" colors for a boat.

"Ideal For Expedition-Type Trips"

One of the challenges with this boat was answering the question of how it was going to offer lateral stability, meaning resistance to leeway. Small boats traditionally use a centerboard or daggerboard in the main hull. That doesn't work on a kayak, of course, because you can't have a centerboard sitting right in the center of the boat where a rider is seated. So we decided to put non-retractable small keels on the amas.

When it came to designing these ama keels we looked at the geometry of the boat and the expected performance of the sail area in order to come up with their size and shape. The surface area of these keels is actually comparable to some of my best racing trimarans. But they only draw about 9 inches of water, so they allow very shallow draft.

The keels are pretty foolproof too. They're built right into the molds when we build the amas. They're a part of the amas. When assembling the craft on a beach or a dock it actually sits very securely on these ama keels. They're incredibly strong and virtually impossible to break off.

We realized that since the windward ama is always going to be up out of the water, its keel wasn't going to cause any drag. The boat's performance to windward with these ama keels is actually quite spectacular. So the keel's design has turned out to be very functional. Sailors seem to be very pleased with how they work.

We also had to come up with a unique solution for the rudder too. Most rudders used on small beach-launching type boats are "kick-up." We didn't want to use a rudder with moveable parts like that because they can be less durable.   So we decided to go with a short, fixed rudder that sits on a large fiberglass shaft.

The rudder is only one foot long and it's built strong enough so that you can rest the weight of the boat on it, and even run the boat into rocks occasionally when sailing, and it will resist breaking. So it's a non-retractable carbon fiber rudder that is strong enough to keep most sailors out of trouble. When kayaking, the *sailing rudder* can either be removed or replaced with a smaller *kayaking rudder* that we also make for these boats.

We developed the sails for the Little Wing in concert with *Doyle Sails* (**www.doylesails.com**). The mainsail is a square head with a fully elliptical roach. Robbie Doyle suggested that we go with a square-headed mainsail because this kind of sail has become very popular among development classes and it offers very good performance for a boat like this. It offers extra sail area, among some other features. The sail shape even looks like a "wing."

More Small Trimarans

The mainsail fits onto the mast very easily. You raise it with a halyard and then pre-tension it very hard to a point where the mast bends a little. The sail will then assume the shape in which it was designed. The square head on this sail is almost like a gaff rig.

There is no boom on this sail either. We decided to go with a boomless sail for reasons of weight, cost and safety. Doyle Sails felt like they could design a sail for this boat simply by using a batten at the foot of it instead of a boom. They were right. It works very nicely.

The kayak features storage hatches, both fore and aft. Most of the high-end kayaks have a bulkhead right behind the space where the rider is seated and one right in front of their feet. This allows room for these storage areas. The bulkheads were originally created for safety, such as when a boat might flip over. These sealed areas prevent water from flooding the whole boat in case water does get inside the cockpit.

This boat offers enough room for users to take light gear with them and go out for a week of camping with no problem. The sailors just have to pack efficiently. The 15.5 Little Wing is ideal for expedition-type trips like this ... in addition to daysailing.

We also offer optional trampolines that fit right onto the boat. If an owner wants to use their Little Wing for an expedition type of trip then trampolines will give them extra room to lash gear onto. We've even had a few of our customers tell us they're planning to use this boat for a trip down the *Intercoastal Waterway*.

Using trampolines would also allow the sailor to get out of the cockpit and stand up in order to stretch their legs. One thing to remember is that the rudder is pedal controlled. So if they want to steer the boat while being out of the cockpit they'll need to get a tiller.

If somebody wanted to bring someone else along for a ride, or even their dog, then the trampolines would be able to handle another adult even though the weight capacity of the boat is specifically designed for one person.

We are currently working on a new 2-person Little Wing trimaran model. We've had a lot of interest expressed in a double version. The target date for availability on the market is 2011. It'll be a 20-foot double kayak with a separate sailing kit. Its mast, sails and amas will all be a bit bigger than they are on the 15.5 model.

"Feeling That You're Going Fast"

The overlying theme of this boat is "ease-of-use." It allows you to quickly get out on the water with little hassle. A lot of small boats are difficult to transport and they just take too long to set up. When that happens then people stop using them.

This boat's light weight, however, doesn't just make it easy to transport. It aids every aspect of its performance. The lightness of the amas at each side allows the boat to turn on a dime. You can see video of the boat on our website where the boat just swings right around almost effortlessly. We can tack it from one beam reach to another beam reach without any problem. The boat just goes right around and then accelerates in the other direction.

We occasionally have first-time sailors come into our shop and we set up a Little Wing for them to test sail. We give them some instruction and then send them out. They might blow a tack at the beginning, but after about 15 minutes of sailing it they're tacking 100% ... they don't get into irons. It's that easy to sail.

As we developed this product we wondered whether or not it would be a boat that beginners could use in order to learn how to sail. So when it was first ready we invited a couple of people who had never sailed before to try out the boat. We gave them some instructions and then sent them out in light wind. We got out on the water beside them in kayaks to see how they would do. It turned out that nobody had a problem sailing the boat. Each person was able to sail on a reach, going downwind and even going upwind.

The Little Wing has turned out to be quite an amazing little personal boat. We've had interest in this boat from all over the world. We recently sold one to somebody in France.

If you check out any of the other videos on our website that feature the Little Wing you'll see one showing Bill Springer. Bill is one of the senior editors at *Cruising World Magazine*. When he showed up to test sail this boat he didn't seem to be very enthusiastic about small multihulls. There wasn't a lot of wind either, but he decided to take the boat out anyway.

When he got into the boat the wind picked up and started blowing in the range of 8–12 knots. You can look at the video and see his reaction for yourself. He was absolutely blown away. He was grinning from ear to ear. We almost couldn't get him to come back in. ☺

An Interview with Ted & Zac Warren

When we first test sailed this boat we put it into the water, sheeted in, and then our jaws dropped. The boat took off so fast we just couldn't believe it. There were a bunch of people at the shore too and we could see the look on their faces. Everyone was amazed. The thing just ripped out of there like it was on steroids. So we've been very pleased at what a great personal boat this has turned out to be.

Sailing can be fun, whether you're out in a Formula 40 catamaran or a little 3-meter trimaran. A smaller boat like the Little Wing is a lot more convenient and less demanding though. To be able to have something this handy and light is very enjoyable.

You can get into a big boat, sheet it in, and get things right, but the relative speed is always slower because the speed potential goes up as the square root of the waterline length. A boat that is twice as long as another may only go about 40% faster based upon the relative size of the boat. So you can get a speed-thrill in a smaller boat that you can just never get in a large boat.

The Little Wing's speed potential, in ideal conditions, is around 15 knots. We exceed 10 knots in this boat pretty regularly. It's quite a feeling to go that fast when you're seated 2 to 3 inches below the water in a kayak like this. As far as pure sensation goes, there is nothing quite like it.

....

For more about the "*Little Wing*" Trimaran visit
http://www.warrenlightcraft.com/
Contact information for Ted & Zac Warren can be found at this website.

OutRig!

Jim Brown's Online Multihull History Project

The Ancient, Modern and Ongoing History of Trimarans, Catamarans and Proas on Display ...

- ➤ The Origins of Modern Multihulls
- ➤ Personal Accounts of Modern Multihull Pioneers
- ➤ Design, Construction & Operation of Modern Multihull Vessels
- ➤ Essays & Featured Stories by Jim Brown & Others
- ➤ Outrig News & Events
- ➤ Seafaring Literature & Multimedia
- ➤ Timeline of Multihull History & Lore
- ➤ Rare Video, Audio & Print Materials
- ➤ A Place to Share *Your* Multihull Story

Visit **www.smalltrimarans.com/r/outrig.html** and catch the wave to Jim's Outrig sailing community.

Chapter 13

An Interview
with Mike Waters

Designer of the W17
& W22 Trimarans

*(**Editor's Note:** This chapter was written entirely by Mike Waters after being invited to contribute to this book.)*

Well I guess I'm now one of the "old guys" in this field but like many of my generation, still passionate about small boats and especially multihulls. When we started 40 plus years back, everyone else who sailed looked down upon them, and it was tough - so we had to be both very convinced and very convincing! But today, cats and tris are finally recognized for what they are, so when we realize that whether we like it or not most of our wild adventure days are over, we want to share our experience and knowledge with others before it's all disappeared 6ft under. That for me was the main drive behind starting my website where I've chosen to zone in on small trimaran design.

I already feel sad that inspirations like Norm Cross and Lock Crowther are not still around. They both contributed so much to the modern multihull ... as has Dick Newick, Derek Kelsall, Jim Brown, John Marples and others; even James Wharram with his minimalist designs that still managed some amazing voyages on a shoe-string. I am pleased to hear that at least a couple of them will be contributing to this book and also, therefore, honored to share my thoughts within the same pages.

Today we have some wonderful boats from the likes of John Shuttleworth, the Quorning Bros, Chris White, Richard Wood, Ian Farrier, Hughes, Tennant etc. (and forgive me if I've forgotten someone important). But it's the "pioneers" that had to be especially effective and convincing, as today's' young sailors have NO idea how resistant the sailing public was to ANY sort of multihull ... and how the press made it especially hard to get the message across that they were safe enough for long voyages when well designed and intelligently sailed.

As others have said before, one glance at an overturned multihull was all the press needed to jump on the concept, without any word of how effective the boat then was as a life raft! A sinking monohull left no trace and so was largely ignored, as the press had nothing to show. But with all the important cross-ocean and round-the-globe records now being held by multihulls, there is no longer that huge hill to climb when presenting a new boat design to the sailing public. Multihulls are now here to stay and if it were not for marina space and multihull cost, might even put pressure on monohull survival!

"My Conversion"

Let me share a little of how I personally got involved. Although I was working towards a career in music at the time in the UK, a casual sailing trip in a 14' gunter sloop when I was 10 led me to reading Arthur Ransome's great adventure stories about 2 intrepid sailing families from the Lake District. After reading

An Interview with Mike Waters

Swallows and Amazons at the age of 11, a chum and I each built a small 10' dinghy and yes, like a thousand other small boats in the UK at the time, they were inevitably named *Swallow* and *Amazon* and our own adventures followed. By the time I was 18, the decision was cast in stone and I gave up dreams of being a concert pianist to study naval architecture and have since created a plethora of designs -- from an 8' pram dinghy to 600' cargo liners.

I left England after graduating from what is now one of the most highly acknowledged boat-design institutes in the world (Southampton Technical University). Then I spent 40 years designing ships of all types for a major shipyard in Canada.

But small boats were always prominent in my life and I first toyed with a cruising catamaran design in the mid 70's ... and rather uniquely at the time, my *Flying Wing* concept featured a lower hull solepiece of fiberglass that was combined with topsides of ply for easy fairing. I mention this, as rather interestingly, this feature has returned in the design of my latest W22 trimaran.

As well as my career as a naval architect for a large Canadian shipyard, which involved many interesting trips overseas to meet potential owners, I started 3 small boat companies and later, a consulting firm called Interface Marine Inc. Now retired (though not from sailing or designing) I am happy to share over 60 years of diverse boat experience (about ½ that time with multihulls) through my website and various consulting activity.
(See www.SmallTrimaranDesign.com).

One may well ask, with a grounding in "conventional" naval architecture etc, why was I was drawn to multihulls along the way? Well, although I can still enjoy sailing almost anything that uses the wind to propel it (and still love my Div-ll sailboard), it was the technical aspects that ultimately led me to accept that multihulls "just made so much sense."

While looking at the monohull concept, it started to bother me that they only reached maximum stability when laid flat over with sails in the water. Once there, they were all too easily flooded and then would sink. Further, when there was a good sailing breeze, this lump of steel or lead on the bottom did little to resist heeling until it was well inclined off center ... so it was doomed to sail at large angles with a greatly distorted underwater hull shape virtually all the time there was a decent breeze. Then there was the additional fact that the boat had to be significantly larger below the water merely to support and float this keel weight, even when it was doing virtually nothing until the boat inclined. And finally, this larger underwater volume made it hard to design a really fine hull shape for higher speeds, unless the boat was also very long. (Mind you, since those days things have changed a bit too. New, higher strength materials have permitted monohulls to sail more like huge dinghies with much greater basic stability than ever before, thereby pushing ultimate speeds up towards the realm of multihulls, though at very high cost and physical demands.)

I had read *Multihull Magazine* since its first issue and also subscribed early on to the UK-published *AYRS Bulletins on Yacht Research* that provoked new ideas and thoughts about boat design. I also attended the first *World Symposium on Multihulls* (in Toronto, Canada) and enjoyed listening to and meeting many of the well-known designers of that time who were of my generation.

So as a result, my interest in multihulls just grew and grew and I have to admit that I was drawn to trimarans even more than catamarans, although both have their place *et raison d'etre*. (For me, a trimaran sails as "a perfect catamaran." ;-) It always has the heaviest hull to windward, and even more, there's an airborne outrigger out beyond that, like the sliding seat on an International Canoe!]

The smaller, "potentially ownable" boats really caught my imagination though. As for all boats, the fun is frequently inversely proportional to their size.

More recently, I have often been asked, what is the biggest appeal of sailing small trimarans as opposed to sailing other types of small sailboats? To this I would reply that a good trimaran design offers the thoroughbred feel of handling a finely balanced racing dinghy with the added attributes of efficiency, power, space, speed and great stability. In many cases, it's drier and more comfortable too!

" So What Is My Typical Design Process?"

Personally, the first thing I do is to *identify the target user and the attributes that I want the boat to excel in.* Exactly what these are and how to achieve them is based on my experience with sailing other designs, and also what I have learned from many others in the multihull design field whom I have had the pleasure to know and who have shared their accumulated and diverse knowledge. All this is tempered and put in perspective by my own technical studies and acquired knowledge, something that I have indeed found quite valuable, as every design is ultimately a collection of difficult compromises, all tailored towards the target attributes and user.

Being someone who graduated in the late 50's, most of my design work has been done using manual methods rather than computers. While the new generation may find this antiquated, my defense would be that to work as we did, we really needed to fully understand all the calculations, what was meant by the figures and how we got there. Most of the great trimaran designers of the past (Brown, Cross, Crowther, Harris, Kelsall, Newick, etc.) doubtless also worked the same way.

Today's young computer–savvy generation can readily create wonderful 3D renditions of some dream concept, but it's not always apparent that the important calculations and detailed engineering are handled better by any software – the workings and formulae of which are now often blind to the user. Having said that however, I did spend 20 years with a large CAD/CAM department under my wing and still use a computer where I feel it can actually add something significant to my work. One thing all good designers know is that computers are working tools and do not do the thinking or critical decision making, so I still always mentally check things in my head for global accuracy and feasibility. It's still far too easy to just accept computer output data that may not be realistic.

I am presently in the process of designing two small trimarans ...the W22, and a smaller W17 for my personal pleasure. (As I have hinted earlier, "the smaller the boat, the greater the fun" so there's a little intro on the W17 at my website).

After owning and sailing two trimarans designed by the brilliant Australian Lock Crowther, I was fortunate to become the owner of what I personally consider to be one of the finest small trimarans ever created -- the first ever Dragonfly from Quorning Boats in Denmark. She was called *Magic Hempel* and turned both the monohull and multihull worlds on their heads when she won her class in a very rough Round Britain race in 1985. (She is featured in the header at **SmallTrimaranDesign.com**.)

For the first time, here was a multihull that could sail decently to windward, tack on a dime (as well as having a light helm), had great stability and she also kept the crew pretty dry in the process. As a beamier prototype for the Dragonfly 25 and later Dragonfly 800, she was once timed by radar at 25.4k in the Baltic ...not half bad for a 25.5' boat with a small cabin, sleeping 2+2! As she won race after race, the boating magazines raved about her clear superiority for good reason, and although the F-27 appeared later that same year, the Dragonfly was always held in the highest regard in her native Europe ... and that apparently remains true even today. Even 5 times Olympic medal winner Paul Elvstrom owned one and admitted it was the most enjoyable boat he'd ever owned. Although I had personally owned some 20 small boats, nothing compared to this wonderful boat. Sadly, I was pressured to sell her due to a passing health issue, and with over 40 prospective buyers enquiring after her, the sale went all too quickly.

Since then, and with many personal years of experience and acquired knowledge, I have continued to dream of a boat to replace her – something that would retain all the fine points of this great design, yet be easier to rig and handle ashore and less costly to build. The new W22 is to be the outcome of all this, and I am convinced she will be an extremely enjoyable boat to own and sail, for those who feel a fit with the design criteria and what that offers.

Though both these designs strive for fine handling and performance with comfort and dryness, the **W17** by comparison will be a comfortable day sailor ... a trimaran of "beach cat" type ... quicker to build and lower in cost. She will both beach and fold readily, be great for a couple or singlehanded and most important ... be comfortable and sail well! I guess a small Discovery 20 would be one flattering way to describe her. Basic plans will be ready for early Spring 2010 and building help for first-time builders, as close as your email. More on the W17 under "New Design Development" on my website.

"A Preliminary Review Of the New W22 Trimaran Design"

The main target of the W22 design is for those who want a fast responsive boat that is not only fun and rewarding to sail, but that also offers a drier ride than the average small multihull. Rather than giving up most of the boat volume for an enclosed cabin, the basic design will feature a 7' long cockpit for comfortable day sailing with friends, but also have a low cuddy (with sitting headroom) for inside protection during a passing storm or the occasional overnight. The cockpit floor and the under-cuddy area will be just above the waterline, so that these areas can naturally drain any water back from where it came. The boat will also be easily sailed single-handed.

The design is being developed to be both easy-to-build and of relatively low cost, keeping in mind that overall performance in the sailing conditions that sailors typically most enjoy is very high on my list of priorities. And by "overall" performance, I also mean seaworthiness, handling, stability, comfort, dryness, low maintenance, trailerability etc., as well as pure speed. All of this was apparent with the original D25R and here is how she looked.

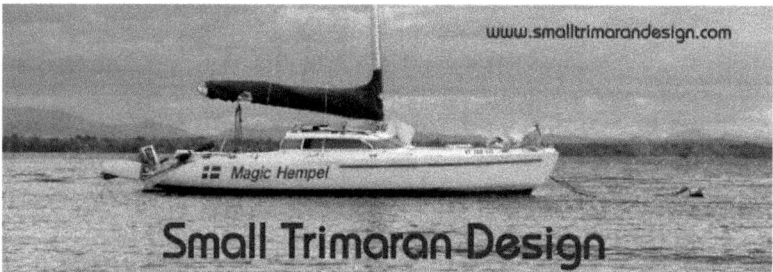

Now for a brief introduction of what the building will involve. All three hulls will be quite rounded in section to give the lowest surface friction possible, though there will also be the option to build the amas using plywood for faster assembly and a slight compromise on speed. The rather unique cross section of the main hull can be seen in this preliminary Body Plan of the W22.

I was recently asked why I did not retain the simple flat sheet form of the W17 hull. My personal thinking is that the W17 is about as large a boat as can justify the simpler form, as the hull cost and construction time becomes a smaller part of the total as size increases. In the case of slightly larger boats (like the W22), I really think it's worth the extra effort to get the lowest resistance possible, so that the overall performance will better match the expense of their larger rig and all the other equipment (mast, fittings, trailer etc) that a boat needs.

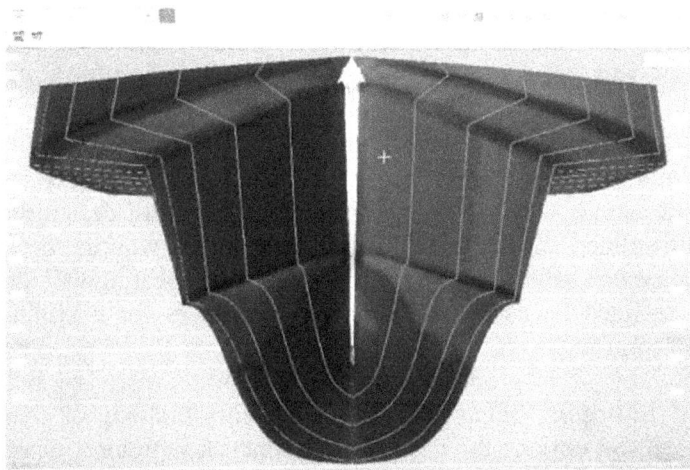

There are a lot of new boats coming out in the 20+ foot range, and having spent a year or more to build one, I think one deserves the best performance one can get. Even the older Discovery 20 is round bilge and for me that makes sense, and resale value will remain much higher for such a boat too. All these factors are less pertinent for a quick-to-build beach tri like the W17, and in that case, getting in the water with the least effort and still having a ball of fun is the reason I intend to build a W17 for myself. Wing masts on both boats will make a difference too.

So back to the W22 -- the main hull will retain the flair just above the waterline that kept *Magic* so dry, provided some extra lift, added to the interior space and also looked good … all without lowering performance. Since *Magic*, many notable designers have adopted this flair. These include UK designers John Shuttleworth & Richard Woods as well as US designer Chris White and French designer Eric Lerouge … all of whose design offerings I have much admired over the years. The underwater sections of all 3 hulls will be targeting the lowest wetted surface possible, combined with a deep forefoot and a straight, somewhat tapered run out to the stern. This is unlike the approach of some designers who have preferred wider, squarer sections and sterns that give more space, but only with higher wetted surface and more low speed drag.

While some claim a wider form might offer a planing ability, I am not one who agrees with that line of thought. (See my website article, *Can a trimaran Plane?*) The overall design will be streamlined and attractive, yet also retain flat working decks that are much safer to move around on. Cockpit seating will also have inclined backs and flat horizontal surfaces for maximum sitting comfort.

Initially, it is proposed that the underwater parts be built using strip-cedar, though the use of cylinder molding or foam core will be options for the amas. I personally prefer a denser wood core for the lower body of the main hull as it provides excellent rigidity with lower material cost than a foam composite. Once a prototype has been built (one on each continent perhaps), the plan is to create a local master-mold for the lower part of the main hull and make a fiberglass lower "solepiece" available for future builders. As this solepiece will also have the important knuckle built-in as well as a substantial vertical centerline girder, it will be extremely stiff and stable in shape and, therefore, well able to guarantee the successful completion of a good looking and high performing main hull. (Most racers will confirm that stiffness equates closely to high performance).

Once the lower curved section is built (either with wood strips or glass), then the easy, fun part can get under way. Basically, the sides are created by rolling plywood around and attaching it to the vertical flange of the lower solepiece.

An Interview with Mike Waters

Temporary framework is set up on the solepiece to guide the placement of the topside plywood, and once in place, temporary gussets will be added to guide the additional extension at the deck level. This is all relatively easy work, as offsets will be provided to define the initial plywood shapes. The plywood sides will simply be lapped over the vertical flange of the lower solepiece and temporarily fixed with sheet metal screws while the joint (of FG matt and epoxy) cures. Once cured, the screws will be removed, the holes filled and the lower edge trimmed off flush with the flare to create a fair knuckle line.

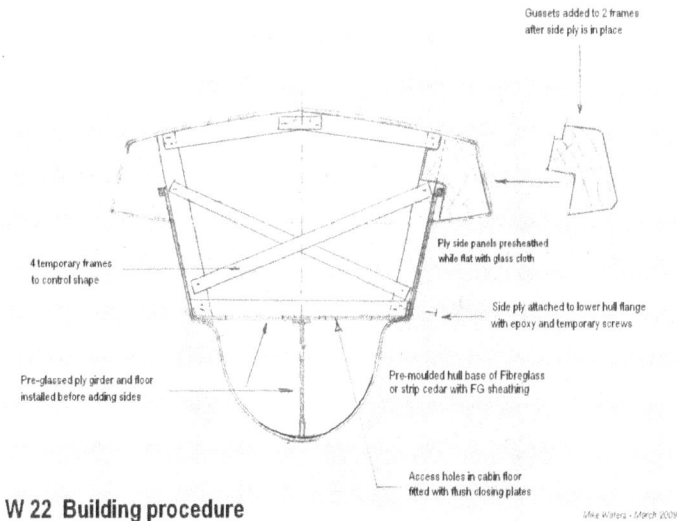

Gussets added to 2 frames after side ply is in place

Ply side panels presheathed while flat with glass cloth

4 temporary frames to control shape

Side ply attached to lower hull flange with epoxy and temporary screws

Pre-glassed ply girder and floor installed before adding sides

Pre-moulded hull base of Fibreglass or strip cedar with FG sheathing

Access holes in cabin floor fitted with flush closing plates

W 22 Building procedure

Mike Waters - March 2009

Note that the interior of the plywood will all be pre-coated with one cloth and epoxy. This very easy step (done while flat and horizontal) will not only provide a far better seal against interior water in the future but will add important stiffness to the panel against exterior pressure. The same approach will be used for the deck panels in both the main hull and amas. Typically the undersides of decks are rarely sealed watertight, and particularly with amas, are very often the initial cause of failure when water gets into uncoated areas while the amas are stored upside down. For both the W22 and W17, that problem will rarely be an issue. As noted earlier, the amas can be built using ones method of choice, though the rounded shape achieved with either cylinder molding, foam or strip cedar, will give the best performance. (Below is a prototype of the proposed shape).

The design will also lend itself to the use of 20' catamaran hulls as amas, if that's an option a builder prefers. However, as these may have less buoyancy than those of W22 design, the ultimate performance may be slightly compromised. The approach of pre-coating the underside of deck panels will also extend to the amas and make for very rapid assembly as well as low future maintenance.

An Interview with Mike Waters

For the initial W22 model that will have demountable akas or crossbeams, a streamlined mast section is specified and preferred. These will simply sleeve into pockets created from layers of glass and be molded and strapped to the ama decks and sides with tows of carbon fiber. This concept has been well tested after I rebuilt the sockets on *Magic* and here is what they finally look like -- very streamlined and professional and quick to use for assembly as no bolting is required.

As long as a demountable trimaran can be set up quickly, with minimal outside help, then it's certainly a very favored approach by many knowledgeable designers. The reason for this is that the beam is not as limited or controlled as it is for most folding systems, and if the beam is too limited, the boat not only heels more than necessary but the boat cannot develop the same power under sail. Heeling can also add resistance, as well as frequently making the boat wetter than need be.

More Small Trimarans

This is not to say "the more beam the better." There are both practical and design limits for overall safety, but in my view, it's just preferable to not have sailing performance held back by the limits of a folding system when that might not be entirely essential. So if you were not confined to daily folding for a marina berth or a narrow launching facility, then I'd certainly take a good demountable into consideration.

Set up time will only be about 20 minutes longer than for a folding system, and the added overall performance (through greater beam and lower weight) for all the hours spent sailing, will more than repay that small inconvenience. And I've not even mentioned the faster build time and lower cost. But there will probably be a slide-out or folding option developed later on for those unfortunates who really need it.

Although a daggerboard can always be accommodated, the base W22 design will incorporate a kick-up board below the cockpit floor. This is because many people will be sailing this boat in shallow inland waters, and at the speeds likely to be developed, a fixed daggerboard could well be the cause of avoidable accidents. (I still remember hitting an uncharted boulder in 8' of water at 6 knots with a nearly vertical dagger board. From the after cockpit, I was thrown totally in the air to land on a cabin-top winch and broke 2 ribs. After that experience, I now design all my dagger boards with a sacrificial tip to ease the impact.) To solve the resistance issues of centerboard slots, the slot will either be kept as short as possible and or have some form of gasket.

Because of the possibility of lifting the main hull significantly and therefore inviting rudder cavitation, the boat has been designed with 2 rudders in mind … one on each ama for maximum control. This also fits with the option of using the hulls from an existing suitable catamaran, as the rudders will come with the hulls, and at the most might need slightly larger blades.

One other interesting thing about the W22 design is that it will include the design of a rotating wing mast that can be built at home. Although no guarantees can *ever* be offered on such designs due to the designer having zero control over both workmanship and the sailing conditions the mast will be subjected to, the design will be of proven heritage and offer significantly improved sailing performance over the more typical rigid, alum stick. Ultimately, the boat's performance will depend greatly on the efficiency of the sails chosen and on the skill and experience of the crew.

In closing this brief review, I will attach a general deck view and sail plan. Although these were sketched out when the design was first being envisaged, they still generally resemble the final design.

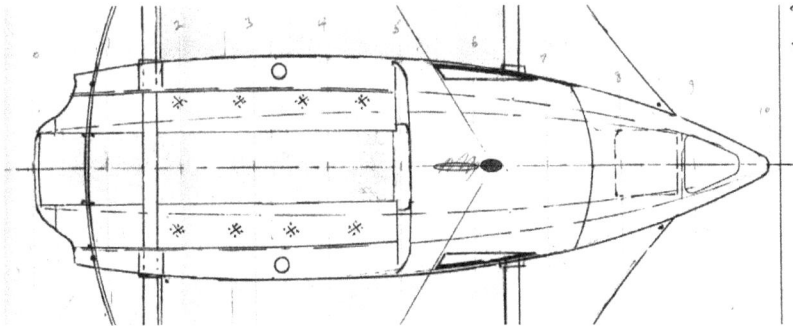

According to the build-time graph included with my Report on Small Trimarans (available through my website), the 3 hulls should take about 400 hours. Depending on the level of skill, experience, tools available etc, the complete boat should take less than 1000 hours. An experienced worker will likely trim down these figures.

Potential owners have sometimes asked me about storage issues. To keep any boat "in optimum condition" requires that it be kept under a ventilated cover as long as possible to protect it from rain, snow, wind abrasion and most importantly, the sun.

More Small Trimarans

As that is not always possible, at least one needs to cover the boat as often as possible.

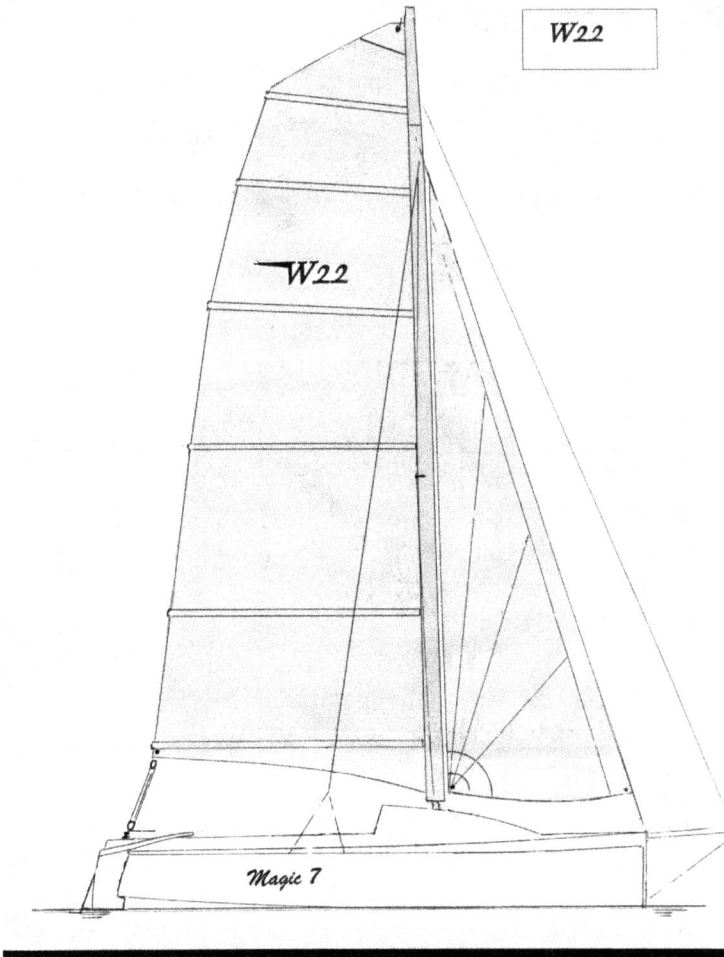

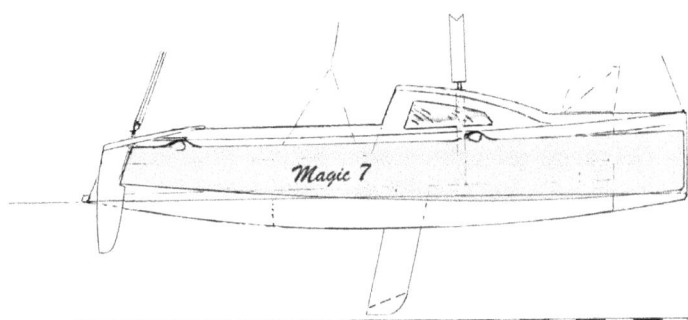

Length:	22ft
Beam:	19ft
Mast Height:	32ft
Sail Area:	310 sqft
Dry Weight:	1000 lbs
Design Disp:	1800 lbs

W22 trimaran preliminary design by Michael Waters 2008

W22

Whilst in use, the boat should be kept clean by freshwater wash-downs and regularly sponged out to keep all internal areas dry. Interiors should also be ventilated and awnings used to cut UV light whenever weather or circumstances permit. In my clearly biased opinion, the major benefits that separate the W22 trimaran design from other small trimarans on the market will be this:

✓ Most bang for the buck – assuming your "bang" matches the chosen design criteria
✓ Greater dryness and overall sailing comfort
✓ A proven concept based on a well tested design, and subsequently "tweaked" by someone with both experience and appropriate knowledge
✓ Attractive looking
✓ Excellent performance in the most typical sailing conditions

So this boat will be for:

- Someone who wants to sail fast with a partner or some friends, yet stay dry and comfortable
- Someone who really appreciates the feel of a thoroughbred at his fingertips and the feeling of high efficiency, even at low wind speeds
- Someone who mostly day sails but occasionally needs protection for camp-aboard trips
- Someone who has the skills and space to build their own boat but not the money for more exotic options like the folding F-22

Although future owners will decide this, its eventual popularity could justify a significant following and this would help retain high resale value. Ideas for a class association are already being discussed.

To help potential boat owners understand more about the materials and design of these fascinating craft, I am happy to refer them to my quasi-technical small-tri website, where about 50 articles are now posted, with more to come. There's no purchasing hype here ... just solid, well-researched data, aimed to inform in as unbiased a manner as my experience permits.

Through my website, one can also submit specific questions that concern potential small-tri builders and owners and I will do my best to answer them as time permits. Those who decide to build to one of my designs will have direct and reasonable access to me through email, to answer any query they may have. And such builders can be confident that my designs have been well thought out, and ultimately offer above average performance.

....

For more about the W17 & W22 trimarans, visit
http://www.smalltrimarandesign.com
Contact information for Mike Waters can be found at this website.

Chapter 14

An Interview with Richard Woods

Owner of Woods Designs & Creator of the Strike 18 Trimaran

Sailing has been a part of my life since I can remember. I was sailing dinghies by the time I was about 4 years old. Sailing was all I wanted to do. My father even built a 6-foot catamaran for me using old oil drums when I was around 5 years old. It had a really little sail on it and I actually have a photo of myself steering this small boat.

These influences led to my interest in dinghies and catamarans. From about 1960 onward, I was never interested in larger monohulls.

I've always enjoyed making things and working out problems. So it was sort of natural for me to try and build a boat. I started building a catamaran when I was about 14 or 15 years of age, but father wisely stopped me from completing it. But when I was 18, I built a dinghy -- an International Moth. (I've built quite a few of them over the years).

My teachers and parents said a person could not make a living being a yacht designer. When I first went to college I studied electronics and electrical engineering and began working for a company that serviced the telephone exchanges in England.

It ended up that I just didn't like working in a factory. And every weekend, I'd hitch a 5-hour ride back home just so I could go sailing for a couple of days before going back to work on Mondays. Then I began sailing for 3 days each week while still in school. It became fairly obvious to me that I wasn't going to become an electronic engineer.

I eventually changed schools and started attending Southampton College of Technology, which is now a university. They had a fairly new yacht design program there. Lots of guys have since gone through their program and gone on to become very well known boat designers. I attended there for 3 years until 1978.

During vacations at yacht school I had the opportunity to work for James Wharram for 2 summers. Then I worked for him during the summer following graduation. I even got to sail his famous boat *Tehini* to the Caribbean. After returning from the Caribbean in 1979, I worked with Derek Kelsall for a year and also built my own boat.

Over the next couple years, from about 1979-1980, I worked with trimarans quite a bit. I also got to sail on a 54-foot trimaran named *Great Britain 4*, which was known as the fastest sailboat in the world at the time. It only had a small engine on it, which made things very interesting when just 2 of us had to bring the boat into a marina.

That boat was very fast in flat water and light winds. It was fun overtaking powerboats in those conditions. Under sail, we'd come up behind a powerboat and before those on board knew what was going on, we'd be alongside them and then overtake their boat. That particular trimaran was horrible in rough weather though. It couldn't go to windward.

There were other trimarans that I worked on at the time, including a design called "*Typhoon*." The Typhoon used the hulls and rig from a Tornado beach cat and combined them with a new main hull. Many plans for that design sold in Switzerland.

Another model came out of that design. It was a smaller, 23-foot version, which utilized the hulls and rig from a Hobie 16. The plans for this 23-footer didn't sell as well as the other boat. I think one reason why is because the Hobie 16 just wasn't a very good boat to use on a trimaran conversion. The hulls' shapes were all wrong and the beam system wasn't suitable.

At that point in my career, aside from some drawings a boat builder once commissioned me to do for 2 or 3 trimarans that were never built, I began concentrating on catamaran designs. It's been that way up until this new trimaran, called the "*Strike 18*."

I've often sailed on trimarans during these intervening years though. This includes boats such as the Dragonfly in England and a few Farrier models in Canada. I've even raced an F-31 and participated in a few local regattas while sailing a Farrier.

"The Strike 18 Trimaran"

The Strike 18 just seemed to me to be an obvious design to draw up at this time. I thought a new kind of beach-cat-to-trimaran conversion was needed. It's actually something I've thought about doing for a while.

The name "*Strike*" originated from one of my previous designs. I have a well-known catamaran model called the "*Strider*." Its name begins with an "s-t," and the sail maker's emblem for the boat was also an "s-t." I also created a dinghy model called the "*Stealth*." Since this new boat is a *tri*maran, I thought about merging the "s" and "t" from previous design names with "tri" and came up with "s-t-r-i" as a basis for this boat's name.

The word "Strike" is short and easy to remember. I sometimes find it difficult to think up names for new boat designs. One of the first names I ever came up with for a design was "*Cockleshell Hero.*" If you write that out a few times, or say it over and over again when talking about the boat, then it doesn't take too long to get fed up with a name like that. ☺

I'd first thought about designing something along the lines of the *Weta*. I think of that as sort of a *geriatric dinghy*. It offers the speed of a high performance dinghy without the need to be quite so energetic. It gets to be harder to sail small boats as one gets older. So a skiff monohull dinghy with outriggers seemed to be a good idea until the Weta Company released their design.

Then I thought about the fact that small catamarans (meaning those less than 20 feet) aren't meant for cruising. It can be uncomfortable sitting on the flat decks of smaller beach cats for long periods of time. The hulls of small cats also have to be small in order to keep their weight down. But that means sailors often end up with the experience of getting very wet or having to trapeze in order to keep the boat stable.

More Small Trimarans

Boats such as the Hobie 17 and 18 have tried to address these issues a bit. They have wings on them that allow sailors to sit up higher and stay drier. Little adjustments like that help keep sailors more comfortable. But in general, if you want a comfortable multihull under 20-feet long, then you have to go with a trimaran instead of a catamaran.

Many trimarans in this size range are very performance-oriented sailboats. The F-22 and the Sprint 750 trimarans, for example, are boats that can be used for racing. I didn't want to design a boat like them for a couple of reasons. First of all, they're very good at being what they are. I saw no reason to try and redo their features. And second, if a sailor has a beach cat then they already possess a boat that can be used to burn around on the water or enter into a race. But if you just want to go out for a nice day sail with family, friends or with children -- without spending a fortune -- then you'll need something else.

An Interview with Richard Woods

In this sense, I was looking to produce a family-friendly cruising design with features similar to the "*Drascombe Lugger*," (**http://www.drascombe-association.org.uk/index.html**) ... except as a trimaran. To do this, my first goal was to create an easy-going sailboat with moderate speed potential. The other goal was to offer a boat that was very simple for individuals to build in their own garage. This means simple to build even for someone who has never built a boat before. So I tried to design this boat in such a way that it's both easy and inexpensive to construct.

The Strike 18 features a flat bottom and can be put together with simple plywood, which will be overlaid with fiberglass and epoxy. A flat-bottomed boat isn't just much easier to build because it has flat surfaces. It's also easier to construct because when you put it on the ground you don't need any supports to hold it up. You can just lay plywood pieces on the ground and then move things around as you build the main hull. A flat-bottomed boat with a chine hull also maximizes cockpit space. The bottom of the boat is essentially the bottom of the cockpit.

Another aspect of having a flat-bottomed boat is that you don't even need a fancy trailer to transport it to the water. I used a flatbed trailer to move my prototype. I just needed a ramp to get the boat onto the trailer and then tied it down with straps, fore and aft, before taking it on the road.

I could have put a round bottom on this model. But if you make rounded corners on a small boat like this, you're really not going to make any practical difference when it comes to reducing wetted surface or improving performance. It would mean putting a lot of extra work into the building process without gaining much benefit.

The fiberglass and epoxy overlaying the outside of the boat is for water-tightness and abrasion. The builder should also lay some fiberglass on the cockpit floor because it's going to get a lot of wear. There will also be fiberglass-taped seams inside the cockpit area. You want to put some glass on the boat's floor because one of the problems with having a plywood boat, depending upon the climate, is that the wood will absorb moisture. That will cause the wood to move slightly, which will eventually cause the paint to start cracking. If the paint cracks then things can become very problematic. If you glass-sheath your wooden boat then you can create an inert surface that will help the paint wear longer.

The reason for sheathing the whole boat is to try and lower its need for maintenance. It takes more effort to build a boat using fiberglass sheathing and epoxy. But in the long-term, it saves lots of time over a period of years. One of my own wooden catamarans was launched in Canada in 1992. It looks like a fiberglass boat because when it was built the whole boat was properly sheathed. It still looks great today. You wouldn't be able to tell it's a wooden boat just by looking at the outside of it.

There are lots of variables when it comes to designing a sailboat. But creating this small trimaran meant I didn't have to worry about making too many compromises. With a bigger boat, many sailors start wanting more accommodations and often become less interested in factors that affect sailing.

The main hull requires 10 sheets of ¼-inch plywood and 10 kilos of epoxy, plus 6-ounce fiberglass sheathing. I used marine-grade gaboon plywood for my boat because it's lighter than fir plywood and also has a nice smooth finish for painting. Boat building suppliers, such as West Marine, sell the specialized materials.

My prototype was built on an island near Vancouver that has 250 people and one shop on it. I'd go into the city of Victoria on Vancouver Island in order to buy supplies from Home Depot. So after one knows what beach cat they're going to use in order to get their floats and rig, then most of your materials for the rest of the boat should be easy to acquire.

"Assimilate Beach Cat Floats"

Years ago, in the mid-60s, a boat called the West Wight Potter (http://www.westwightpotter.com) became popular. These boats come in 14-foot and 19-foot versions. A guy named Stanley Smith, who originally built them in England, developed them. He sailed across the Atlantic during the 1950s in what was basically a fairly small, open boat. He used a dinghy for a cabin roof on it while crossing the Atlantic.

After returning to England, he eventually started building his "Potter" model on the west end of the Isle of Wight, which was influenced by the boats used to bring in the crab pots around that area. His boats feature a unique shape-shear. They're very low at the back of the cockpit, reminiscent of the feature used by the crabbers to bring their crab pots into the boat. But they're high at the front and stern areas in order to be good in waves. This design is essentially an open boat with a little cabin in the middle of it.

My family had a West Wight Potter and it was one of the first boats that I ever sailed with or without the cabin. There were thousands of them commercially produced and sold, especially in the U.K. and U.S. market. They're still a very popular small, trailerable monohull boat. When designing the Strike 18, I thought about how nice it would be for this trimaran to feature a "removable cabin" on it that was similar to those on the West Wight Potters.

My prototype was only built in an "open cockpit" version, without a cabin. But you can see pictures of this boat on my website with a windscreen. Having such a windscreen makes sense because it offers sailors a bit of protection and also forms the front for a removable cuddy cabin. Whether or not a cuddy cabin is ever added to a Strike 18 will depend upon what an individual sailor/builder wants. If a cabin is put on this boat then it will become a small cruiser for someone who is on a very tight budget. If a sailor wants to go single-hand sailing, or putter around lakes, rivers and creeks, then this boat offers a comfortable way for a person to sleep under shelter.

The windscreen structure on my prototype is made out of plywood. This needs to be rigid in order to hold plexiglass windows in place. And when you put the mast up, there are also places on this portion of the boat to hold temporary shrouds that keep the mast in place when you're raising it. None of the windows on the Strike 18 will need to be bigger than 2-feet square. It's very possible a store like Home Depot will carry plexiglass in the size needed to fit the openings.

The windscreen could be made longer in order to create a solid spray hood. It would still allow a big open cockpit, but there would be room for a little cooker and porta-potty in the front of the boat. That would also permit at least 1 person to get under some type of shelter if you're sailing and it starts to rain.

If a family wants to use the Strike 18 for camp-cruising, then I think it's more likely they'll want to have an open version of the boat in order to have more room. They could even build a sort of tent that covers the cockpit area for camping. Or small tents could be set up on trampolines across the beams.

The Strike 18 will ideally assimilate beach cat floats in the 16-to-17-foot size range. I already sell a beach cat design called the "*Quattro 16*," which is a plywood boat constructed in stitch and glue. I used the hulls and rig from that design as the basis for the floats on this trimaran. But the actual outriggers on my prototype ended up coming from an 18-foot-long Morrelli & Melvin catamaran. I don't know how old it was, but I cut the hulls down and shortened them to 16 feet in order to put them on my Strike 18.

Any 16-foot float used as an outrigger for this boat will be in proportion to its main hull. If the floats are 18 feet long then the outriggers will stick out in front of the main hull, which would look a bit strange. It would also make the boat heavier overall.

A Nacra 5.2, for example, would be a good choice because its floats are the right size and it uses 3-inch-diameter crossbeams, which is ideal for this particular small trimaran.

I don't necessarily recommend using a Hobie 16, however, because of the way its beams are fitted. A beach cat with proprietary beams, like the Hobie 16, makes the conversion a little bit harder because the float beam boxes match those specific beams. It would be feasible to have a proprietary beam stub stick out of the beach cat hulls in order to attach another beam onto it and affix the floats to the Strike 18. But like I said, that adds a little bit more work to the construction.

If the sailor wants to keep their beach cat useable as a beach cat, then they'll need a separate set of beams to attach the floats to the main hull of the Strike 18 instead. If the original beach cat's beams are used then they'll be cut and attached to the main hull.   The crossbeams can be made from 3-inch fabricated aluminum or even mast sections.

Old mast sections are usually pretty easy to get because there are places that have broken masts lying around. And spar makers often have various mast pieces leftover after cutting down 40-foot mast sections to smaller lengths. If a builder can acquire 4 of these mast sections in the right length then they'd make ideal crossbeams for this boat. That would also be relatively cheap because the greater expense when it comes to mast sections is putting fittings for sails on rather than the basic extrusion. But since these sections aren't going to be used for sails they won't require costly fittings.

Whatever is used for the beams will attach to the main hull using a horizontal pivot bolt, which is basically a half-inch stainless steel threaded rod.   The vertical connection will then be a 3/8-inch bolt that clamps to the boat. These things will be easy to get at any hardware store.

My prototype features outriggers with daggerboards. So if you have a beach cat with daggerboards then you don't have to build a daggerboard into the main hull, which makes it even easier to build. A minor disadvantage to having daggerboards in the floats is that they tend to catch weeds. This can be very irritating when sailing in places like the Pacific Northwest where there are lots of floating weeds.

A sailor can choose between using the 2 rudders that are on the floats of the beach cat hulls or putting one in the middle of the main hull.   If you keep the beach cat rudders then you'll have to fit the beach cat tiller onto the main hull. This will allow the beach cat rudders to angle inward. If you use a central rudder then many dinghy tillers and rudders used on boats that have 10-inch transoms will fit onto this boat. They're also pretty easy to obtain. I bought mine complete from a consignment store for about $25.

There are videos and pictures on my website that show us sailing in the open cockpit version of the Strike 18. We haven't yet fitted the trampoline nets onto the boat. But when they're attached a sailor will be able to fit a tiller extension onto the boat and sit out on the windward ama. It's also important to add trampolines because if the boat doesn't have them it'll be difficult to board it from a dock.

After trampolines are attached they can simply become a permanent fixture of the boat. The way the crossbeams simply fold up make it ideal to lace trampolines onto them and leave them attached.

The beam on the Strike 18 will be wider than the catamaran the mast was originally used on. The mast will also sit higher on this boat than it would on the cat. So you'll have to lengthen the shrouds on the mast about 18 inches or so when using the beach cat mast on this boat. The easiest way to do that is by using lanyards. The lines will then be attached to the same chain plates that are used for the beach cat configuration. The same thing will have to be done for the forestay.

"Very Easy To Sail"

The Strike 18 is a small boat. But it's certainly made so 4 adults can sail on it comfortably. You may be able to fit a couple of other adults on board. But that would be the maximum number of people for this particular boat. A couple with 2 children would also be ideal for this sailboat.

I remember sailing in a 10-foot dinghy with my family when I was a child. Both of my parents were in the boat with 3 children and our dog. We even sailed this little boat in northern France and took it to Sweden in order to cruise around its islands. We were out all day sailing in the small dinghy and everyone made out fine. So a small family should be quite comfortable if daysailing on the Strike 18.

Setting up the boat in order to go sailing when it's on the trailer is pretty straightforward. The outriggers will be attached to the beams, which only take about a minute to drop down and lock into position. Then the mast goes up. So it should only take about 5 minutes longer to set up than a beach cat.

The outriggers are going to be very light. They're only going to weigh about 80 pounds or so. They don't sit up on the trailer very high either. When they're raised up above the main hull they're simply lashed together when trailering the boat. And the main hull will be tied to the trailer during transport.

This boat is going to be a quick build for most sailors. I estimate that it will only take about 150 hours until the boat is ready to be painted. After that, some guys will spend more time painting, filling, sanding and then repainting than other individuals will take. So the time it takes to finish this boat will vary from sailor to sailor, depending upon how much time they want to take finishing the boat to get it looking like they want it to look. Putting a "boat show" finish on a boat can take a lot more time.

An Interview with Richard Woods

I've often built "50-foot boats," meaning boats that look good when you stand 50 feet away from them. ☺ Seriously though, making the boat strong or seaworthy has nothing to do with whether or not it has a boat show finish.

Beach cats typically have very low booms. Sailors have to constantly duck underneath them. I didn't want a mast at deck level on the Strike 18 because I didn't want sailors to have to duck and experience that constant inconvenience. So when sailors are seated in the cockpit the bottom of the sail will be well above their heads.

Anyone who has ever sailed in the Pacific Northwest has discovered there is often very little wind here in the summer. My first test sails in the Strike 18 took place during a 2-week period this past summer. Those were mostly very light wind days. But my 3rd sail on this boat happened to be a very gusty day. I overheard a couple of other sailors say the gusts were hitting 25 knots at times. There were other multihulls around me – an F-24, a 35-foot catamaran, a 40-foot trimaran and a couple of F-32s – and everyone else was reefed. My Strike 18 was the only one that didn't reef. It sailed pretty steady between 9 and 10 knots … and even hit 11 ½ knots at times.

I was sailing very close to the shore and the hill behind me was about 1,400 feet high. The wind was blowing over the top of the hill and the gusts were coming downward, instead of horizontally. So the wind wasn't ideal for speed. So my guess is that in ideal conditions this boat may occasionally be able to hit 15 knots. In a force 5 gale, on relatively flat water, the boat will probably average between 10 and 12 knots.

The boat will probably sail very gently between 6 and 8 knots in steady wind. When you're sailing like this there will be no spray in the cockpit and there may not even be any other sensation except that you're going along very quickly. The jib I used on these trial runs is probably 35 years old and the mainsail is pretty old as well. So when this boat is fit with good sails it will obviously go along even better.

More Small Trimarans

Lots of people say they want a "fast" boat. I mean, nobody ever says they want a *slow* boat. But what they really want is something that is going to carry all their stuff and is easy to handle. If everyone really wanted a *fast* boat then they'd all get a high-performance racing design.

I've also found that most people aren't as good at sailing as they think they are. Most individuals don't really understand what *sailing fast* means. This is particularly true when it comes to cruising boats. Most sailors would not be able to do the work required to sail on a boat that covers 200 miles in one day. And very few people actually know what sailing at 20 knots is like.

Everyone likes to think every multihull should be able to go 20 knots. But I've told people that 6 knots is like going 60 miles per hour in a car. Going 8 knots is like going 80 miles per hour in a car. But going 20 knots is like going 200 miles per hour in a car. Have you ever done 200 miles an hour in your car?

The highest speed most people will ever be able to go in a car is between 120 and 130 miles per hour. That is about what it feels like going 12 knots in a small boat like this. That would actually be frighteningly fast for most sailors. If you're going between 12 and 15 knots in a boat, especially this one, you're going to know you're going *fast*. For most sailors, achieving 20 knots is really pie-in-the-sky. It's really unrealistic for the vast majority of boats and the vast majority of sailors.

The *Strike 18* offers a very comfortable ride and is very easy to sail. This, in itself, makes it fun. In America, motorboats have tended to be the most popular boats over the years. There are fewer sailboats sold in the U.S. than in many other parts of the world. If you visit places like England or France then it becomes apparent that sailing is huge. There are lots of small craft and lots of beach cats and people enjoy sailing on many bodies of water.

A part of my being a yacht designer came from wanting to design boats that I would love to have myself. I've tried to produce boats that are unique and stand apart in some way from what others have done. I like to design boats and frequently build them and then sell them so I can keep on doing new things.

I often tell people, *"If the boat designer doesn't build, own or sail one of his own boats then why go to that individual for plans?"* I currently own 3 different sailing boats because I like using them for different reasons. I'm on a cruiser right now that we're going to be out on for the next 6 months. But the Strike 18 will be a good boat to take out for a day of fun.

If you don't have to worry about getting into trouble with it or controlling a boat then you're going to enjoy it more. The Strike 18 is a boat that you can point in the direction you want it to go and it goes.

There is a free downloadable study plan for the Strike 18 at my website. It features some more photos of the boat and some drawings. It shows about 90% of this boat's features. So I encourage readers to visit my site and view it. Full building plans for the Strike 18 are also available and are priced very reasonably.

....

For more about the "*Strike 18*" Trimaran visit
http://www.sailingcatamarans.com/
Contact information for Richard Woods can be found at this website.
* Last 4 photos courtesy of Marlene Mackenzie.

Chapter 15

An Interview with Rob White

Owner of White Formula, Builder of the Challenger Trimaran

I got into sailing because my father sailed. His father sailed -
- and his father sailed before him. As a matter of fact, my great,
great grandfather was a guy named Captain Carter, who sailed
the King's yacht *Britannia* during one of the first America's Cup
races.

I head up a company called White Formula and we're boat
builders. My father was a boat builder and my grandfather, who
was mainly an oysterman, also knew how to build boats. So my
family has been a part of various boat-related businesses over the
years.

More Small Trimarans

My father headed up a company called SailCraft at one time and they not only created some nice-sized cruising cats, they also produced boats that won races and held world speed records. There was once a very popular 30-foot cruising catamaran model called the *Iroquois*. SailCraft built about 300 of those sailboats during one 8-year period. That was quite a thing back then.

Over the years and through various recessions our family's marine-based businesses changed and adapted. We eventually started building Tornado catamarans and we've sort of stayed with smaller boats ever since. I've personally built all kinds of boats though.

I worked as a technical director for a company called *Topper Sailboats*, which make a variety of fiberglass models. *Topper* now has a dinghy named after them that is a popular 13-footer here in England. You'll frequently see them up around lake areas in the U.K.

The *Topper* dinghy is made out of a plastic developed by a company named ICI. The *Toppers* had originally been made out of fiberglass and then, about 25-30 years ago, they started making them in Injection Moulded Polypropylene. As a matter of fact, Topper is launching its first 16-foot catamaran. There is also a planned 12-foot catamaran too.

As a result of my involvement with *Topper* we also started making a range of different types of boats here at *White Formula*. We were quite successful. We sort of broke the mold on a number of newer designs, including more performance-oriented boats.

I've sort of gone back to creating resin-molded boats nowadays though. We try and make all kinds of boats available to families that want to go sailing. And I really like the fact we've got back into multihulls.

An Interview with Rob White

"I'd Just Love To Be Able To
Go Off Sailing By Myself"

The Challenger trimaran actually came about during the time my father had his SailCraft business. There was a lady named Diana Campbell, who was the granddaughter of a gentleman named Sir Donald Campbell. He was a famous guy who once held 13 world speed records for powerboats and cars. There was obviously a bit of money in that family. His boats and cars were named *Bluebird*.

I can't recall exactly what it was, but Diana had some sort of disability. Her body was very "locked up." Many of the bones in her body had trouble moving and she was very physically disabled. I got to know her when I was about 20 years old while working in the family business.

Back around 1977-78 our family's business used to produce a boat called the *Apache*, which was a 40-foot catamaran. Diana used to come to our shop and sit out on this boat because it had a lot of space and there was room to put her wheelchair on.

As one of these Apache catamarans was being built one day she said, "*I'd just love to be able to go off sailing by myself.*" The designer of the Apache was a man named Rod McAlpine Downie. He was a friend of my father's and he said to Diana, "*Well, I can design something for you.*"

Diana literally couldn't move her hands. She hardly weighed anything at all; she was almost like a Barbie doll. I'd pick her up when she came to our workshop and take her up a wooden ladder so she could be taken aboard the boat. But she just longed for the freedom to be able to sail by herself even though she was disabled.

Rod decided that the best sailboat he could design for Diana would be a trimaran because it could be both stable and fast. And that was the start of the sailboat that is now known as the *Challenger* trimaran.

So it was SailCraft that built the first Challenger. Nobody thought the boat would ever go into production. It was just something we wanted to do for Diana so she could go off and sail by herself, without being totally dependent upon other people.

Diana didn't want to sail a monohull because she thought they were slow and boring. But this little tri had light sheet loads and allowed her to go off and really enjoy herself. She had freedom when she sailed it. It gave her an opportunity to feel like she had some part of her life back.

The original boat we build for Diana is basically the same boat we offer right now. It's 4.57 meters LOA, has a 3.5-meter beam and it weighs just 145 kilos (*320 lbs*).

Even though we didn't think this boat would become a production model we made molds for it. Since Diana wanted the boat in fiberglass we just created molds so we'd have them in case the sailboat ever needed to be replaced in the future. Her family had the means to afford a custom-made fiberglass boat for her.

An Interview with Rob White

The Challenger's hull form has pretty much stayed the same since then, although the original design featured a rolled gunnel. You know how a Laser is put together, with the deck and hull rolled over, with a flange around it? The Challenger was like that originally. It's different now though. Now it looks sort of like a Tornado hull, where everything is flush.

"Minutes To Put Together"

The fiberglass hulls require no special care and the center hull is self-bailing. If any water comes in when sailing then it'll go right out the back again.

The Challenger is easily trailerable because it comes apart very easily. The whole sailboat is held together by 2 crossbeams that are held in place by 12 bolts. It only takes about 5 minutes to take apart and only about 10-15 minutes to put together when setting the boat up to go sailing.

More Small Trimarans

Each boat comes with a mainsail. There is no headsail. The performance is still very good though.

The mast is aluminum construction with a carbon top. It's one of the latest developments for this product. The mast is similar to a Laser sailboat. It just slides into a socket in order to set it up.

The boom is slightly raised so sailors don't have to constantly bend over when sailing in the cockpit. It sits well above their heads.

We can tailor make the boat to suit individual sailor's needs. The seats are made to be adjustable. And since there are all types of physical disabilities we uniquely rig each boat with foot or hand controls or install a winch with power control. We can also set things up more conventionally. Everything depends upon what the sailor wants.

There are 2 questions I always get asked about this trimaran. People basically want to know, "*How stable is the Challenger?*" and "*What kind of performance can I get out of this boat?*"

There is no rigging on the mast. It's totally self-supporting. If a sailor gets a real strong gust of wind they can just release the mainsheet. Then the mast will just go to weather all around. This is a safety feature that prevents capsizing and keeps sailors from coming to harm.

If a sailor presses the boat too much, its leeward hull will go into the water and that will cause the sail to spill wind. This also works to prevent capsizing. I wouldn't say there is no chance of capsizing this boat ... after all, there were those who said the Titanic wouldn't capsize, but it did. In my opinion, however, there is very little chance of it happening with a Challenger.

This sailboat handles really well. It tacks and gybes nicely and can be sailed really hard. A few of these boats have actually been pushed near 18 knots on a close reach. They move along pretty good.

The Challenger is a production model and comes to customers as a complete boat. It's offered as a complete package that is ready-to-go. And our company can fix any boat or replace any hardware if it becomes necessary.

More Small Trimarans

We've been building these boats for a while. And we get orders for a number of them each year. Most of our business comes by word-of-mouth. We don't even have a brochure for it. We just build them on a made-to-order basis.

One of our goals is to keep costs down as much as possible because we don't want these boats prohibitively expensive to sailors who want to acquire them. It's fairly expensive to make each boat because they're not in full production and we don't seek to make a lot of money on this product. Some Challengers are purchased for individual sailors through fundraising efforts.

We've actually exported a few boats outside of the U.K. We've shipped to places like Greece, France, Holland, Portugal, Spain and Germany. A couple of Challengers have even been sent to Canada. We haven't shipped any to America yet. But I think it's just a question of finding the right person at the right time.

It usually takes about 3 weeks for us to construct a boat after getting an order. This typically includes the time it takes to set up the controls for each unique customer. For example, if a person wants controls just on the right side of the boat then we'll do that. Or they might require foot or hand steering; we can do that too. Other sailors request electronic motors for controls. So anything can be custom-made to fit what an individual sailor might want.

If anyone looks up information about the Challenger on the Internet they'll probably come across a few web pages that talk about a fellow named Daniel and *Daniel's Dream*. Daniel was a lad around 20 years old who had cancer and just physically couldn't sail a conventional boat. His dream was to get this boat into the Para-Olympics.

Daniel inspired a following that has been pursuing this goal. Even though they haven't succeeded yet, I heard they might be getting close to achieving the funding and votes necessary to make it become a reality. I never met Daniel, who passed away a few years ago, but I do know his father. And he is a part of the effort to eventually make Daniel's dream come true.

"A Blood Rush"

The Challenger is a very simple boat. Yet it's fast and very exciting. It's a blood rush for anyone who sails it. And this is true whether the sailor is handicapped or not.

It's really fun for Challenger owners to sail and compete against others. When these boats get together for races here in the U.K., able-bodied sailors often compete against sailors with disabilities on an equal basis. And Challengers also appear in other multihull races as well. Everyone in the sailing community really enjoys getting together for Challenger events.

Producing these boats is really a fulfilling thing for our company to be involved with. It gives us a sense that we're able to offer something special to certain sailors who are physically challenged in some way.

There is a sailing center over here in the U.K. that was originally built to host Olympic-type sailing events. Our government purchased it about 12 years ago. A group of Challenger sailors met there recently for a day of sailing and everyone had a blast. And even though these boats have turned out to be ideal for sailors who are physically challenged (either as a result of accident or sickness) most small multihull lovers love sailing Challengers.

The sailors who are interested in this boat want an adrenaline rush. We've even had guys buy this sailboat who used to do powerboat racing. They don't want to sail slow boats. Sailing at

14-15 knots is pretty exciting for most people. And these guys have a rush when sailing the Challenger.

After reworking some things on the design a while back, I took a Challenger out for a sail and was amazed by how well it performed. I've been a part of championship sailing teams when I was younger and sailing this boat was still quite thrilling.

....

For more about the Challenger Trimaran visit
http://www.whiteformula.com
Contact information for Rob White can be found at this website.
* Copyrights to all pictures used in this chapter belong to the
Challenger Class Association, and are used with their
permission. David Newton took photograph #1. Photographer
Marcia Carpenter took pictures #3, #6, #7 & #8. Photographer
Nick Smith took pictures #2, #5 & #9. And photographer Anne
Larr took photo #4.

Chapter 16

An Interview with John Marples

Owner of Marples Marine & Designer of the CC Cyclone 23 Trimaran

My family immigrated to New York from Great Britain in 1950. We lived in a house with a little lake next to it and I helped my father build an 8-foot Hagerty Seashell. It was a kit boat – very much like an El Toro. I ended up spending a lot of time in that boat and had lots of fun with it. But I didn't really get into boats until I was in college.

I went to college in San Luis Obispo, which is now California Polytechnic State University. A future boat designer named Bill Lee, who coined the term "*fast is fun*," was my college roommate. He went on to design boats under the *Santa Cruz* line (including the SC27, SC50, SC70 & the 67' Merlin).

Another college buddy had a 15-foot Snipe sailboat. We had a lot of fun in the sailing club at school. It was like having the same kind of fun on the water that I'd enjoyed as a kid.

After first studying to be an aeronautical engineer, I finished up college as a mechanical engineer because the airplane business had crashed in the early 1960s. I didn't want to have to try and look for a job in an industry that had no jobs available after getting out of school. But I wanted to build either a boat or an airplane after graduation. Since I couldn't live aboard an airplane I decided to build a boat.

"The Inclination To Be A Designer"

About this time, I met Jim Brown. He came to a local yacht club and gave a talk one night and I'd gone to hear him. We struck up a friendship and I ended up becoming one of his first clients. He hadn't been in the design business very long at that point.

I tried to get Jim to redesign one of his earlier models for me. But he convinced me that one of his newer boats at the time – the *Searunner 37* – would be ideal for my boat-building project.

So I built the 37-footer and had a really good time with it. I ended up living aboard that boat for about 10 years and even set a corrected time record in the '72 Transpac. A couple of years were also spent cruising around the South Pacific.

I ended up selling my Searunner after going back to California in order to fund my re-entry into a land-based business operation. The money enabled me to buy a house and start up my own design office.

From the onset, it seemed like the inclination to be a designer came very naturally to me. And building that first boat when I got out of school had been a fun pastime. By applying the knowledge I'd learned at school I had a small business manufacturing hardware for certain boats, including hatches, cleats, ports and running backstay/forestay levers and all kinds of things. Before going cruising on the Searunner 37, I'd sold the business to a friend. It paid for me to be able to go sailing for a while, so things worked out.

The lifestyle of building a boat and then cruising opened up the opportunity for me to have a vibrant business in those years. Lots of people wanted to build boats and various designers sold tons of plans. All sorts of boats were being constructed with a wide range of materials, including wood, metal and ferro-cement. But the multihull portion of that activity was a significant percentage of it. It just sort of seemed natural for me to get involved with it.

Jim was selling a series of *Searunner* models, including 25', 31', 37' and 40'. We realized there was a large gap between the 31-footer and the 37-footer. There seemed to be a need for a midsize boat in between those 2 sizes. Jim was very busy and he'd already designed a number of boats, plus had written 2 books. He wasn't enthusiastic about sitting down at the drawing board in order to design a new boat. He did agree with me that a new multihull in that size range was a good idea so he challenged me to draw it. He then offered it in the design line as co-designers.

That led us to take stock of the entire Searunner series. I generated all of the necessary mathematical backgrounds, ratios, strengths and buoyancies for Jim's existing boats. Then I designed the Searunner 34.

The 34-footer ended up being a project that both Jim and I had ideas for. We ended up with a fairly sophisticated boat. If any criticism could be given, somebody might have said it was *too strong* and *over-designed*. We'd done that because we'd just gone back and looked at the previous designs and improved them a bit. We did this redesign work on all of the Searunner boats in the series.

Jim and I noticed that Wharram catamarans were selling very well during the mid '70s. So we decided to add another series of boats that were even simpler to build than those in the Searunner series because simplicity was a part of what attracted boat builders to the Wharram designs.

Searunners are good sea boats because they're heavily compartmentalized on the inside. That helps sailors nicely organize them for sea voyages. But they may be too sophisticated to build for some individuals. This would be especially true, for example, for those who look at simple designs, such as the Wharram catamarans, and are attracted to them. I think the Searunners can sail rings around those cats. But the cats' simple design and construction were attractive to many sailors that wanted to build a multihull. So Jim and I came up with another design series we called *Seaclipper*.

Seaclipper 28

An Interview with John Marples

The Seaclippers are much more simplified in their construction. They usually don't have any wing structure in them at all. They feature a tubular main hull, which houses the main living space. (The bigger boats in this series were lengthened in order to include ample living area). The result, however, is a boat that is much easier to build.

Building a Seaclipper requires fewer parts and is a bit less expensive than building a Searunner. The 28-footer was the first model. Jim and I designed it together. Then I went out and expanded that series to include a 34', 38' and 41'. These were the first 4 boats in the Seaclipper line.

It took me a long time before I gave in and finally designed the Seaclipper 16. I'd get calls asking for a 16-foot trimaran and I'd think, "*Why do you want to build one that size?*" I'd tell these guys they could go down and buy a used beach cat for less than the cost of materials needed to build a 16-foot trimaran.

After repeated requests, however, I finally designed the 16-footer. It turned out better than I'd originally imagined. The Seaclipper 16 includes plans for an optional Hobie 14 rig, which includes a jib. If a builder finds a Hobie 14 rig they can plunk it right on top of the boat, without any modifications, and go sailing. If not, then my plans include a specific, tapered, wood-section mast for it. To build it, you'd make a solid wood mast and then plane it down to create a tapered piece of wood that offers the bending characteristics it ideally should have.

The guys at *Duck Flat Wooden Boats* in Australia sell Seaclipper 16 plans. They found a mast maker who gave them a tapered aluminum section to use for its mast. That turned out to be a very nice way to go for the boat. Whichever kind of mast one chooses, a builder can scavenge around for parts off boats of similar size in order to fulfill rigging needs and save a good bit of money in the process.

"The 3-Meter Tri"

The 3-meter tri is another one of my designs. It's a little 10-foot-long harbor racer. It's become a popular little boat. We've sold a ton of plans in Australia. This little tri even became a racing class that was started when I lived in the Seattle area. I've even made modifications to them for disabled sailors. These boats have been rigged with steering handles (instead of standard steering pedals) along with other modifications. They're very fun. When Jim Brown went sailing in a 3-meter tri for the first time he said all he could do was laugh the whole time.

The actual necessity for this boat design was very different from what may appear. I'd been doing a lot of boat shows at the time and had a folding 26-footer on a trailer that I was taking with me to show prospective customers. I traveled all over the northwest showing the 26-footer. But it was hard generating interest in our models because the 26-footer was either tied in the water or folded up on the trailer. So I decided to build a boat that was almost like a model, but also big enough that somebody could get in and sail around in it during the shows.

I created a 10-foot model boat because 10 feet seemed to be a logical length. It was small, but it gave me something I could handle and use for a display. But it was also just big enough to offer decent performance while sailing around in it.

Over the years, we've worked on this 3-meter design a little bit and they now go upwind at about 4 ½ to 5 knots. Off the wind, they sometimes exceed 6 knots. Think about going that fast in a little boat like this. It almost gives the same sensation as if you were doing 30 knots in a 40-footer.

If you're sailing in choppy waters then waves may jump into the boat with you periodically. You can fit this boat with little piston bilge pumps attached to the centerboard trunk (right between your legs) to pump the bottom of the cockpit dry if you get an accumulation of water inside.

Everything done to that boat, every little adjustment made, really affects the way it handles. It really trains a sailor to be vigilant about their sail trim and everything else regarding the boat. Just the right tweaks here and there can make the boat go faster and sail a little bit better.

Tweaking the sails on a 3-meter tri will help the sailor figure out little details when it comes to racing a boat and getting it to go faster. It's very helpful and also makes it a very good boat for learning how to sail.

You obviously can't shift your weight around much in the 3-meter tri. You can move your weight around in the cockpit but you can't improve performance by hiking out onto an ama. Hiking out isn't allowed for this racing class.

It's also great because you can concentrate on tweaking the performance of this little trimaran without having to worry about capsizing it. And steering becomes almost second nature after a while … almost like driving a car. You don't even realize you're doing it. The rudder pedals on this boat allow you to turn right or left without thinking about it too much.

The 3-meter tri is challenging to learn how to sail *well* though. This is a point that was driven home to our northwest racing fleet one day. Our fleet had existed for a couple of years and we got Jack Christiansen, one of the best sail makers and sailors in the Seattle area to do some developmental work on the mainsail. We invited Jack to go out racing with our fleet.

We all thought we were pretty good at sailing these boats. Our fleet didn't have anyone in it that won all of the time. It seemed like we each took turns winning at different times. On the day that sail maker came and sailed with us, however, he easily walked away from all of us. We just couldn't believe it!

"*How did he do that?*" we all wondered. "*We've been sailing these things for 2 years now and I thought we're getting really good at it. But this guy just hopped in one of our boats and took off and left us in the dust.*" It took us a while to get over the shock.

Jack really showed us that we actually had a lot to learn when it came to sailing those boats. He was a sail maker who was also an exceptionally good sailor. He knew what the sail trim should look like and it really enhanced his performance. That event always sticks in my mind as one of those pivotal things that can happen just when you're feeling pretty good about what you do. You may think you're pretty good at something and then somebody else can come along and just leave you in the dust.

There is no spinnaker pole on the 3-meter tri, but there are 4 strings that control the spinnaker sheets. There are lots of ways each sail can be adjusted and tweaked. There are various controls for the mainsheet. I used a downhaul and outhaul and other controls on my boat to tweak the sheets in order to try and get the sails to look exactly a certain way. The last 3-meter tri I owned had a dashboard with 13 strings coming into the cockpit, which allowed me to make all kinds of sail adjustments. This is a part of the fascination with sailing these boats.

The 10-footer features an aluminum, 3-section telescoping mast that is a little "bendy." It now has its own dedicated rig, which features a mainsail and a spinnaker. There are no stays on it. It's a little different from what you'd see on a planing dinghy. The way the mast bends and shapes the sail in order to affect airflow will be somewhat unique for this design.

I've given the sail on this boat 2 more feet of hoist since it was originally designed. It's now almost 16 feet tall, so the sail is about 1 ½ times the length of the boat. It's a big rig for the boat and the sails perform really well in light airs. You can also reef it down for higher wind.

When somebody builds a 3-meter tri I give them specs for the various sizes of pipe they need to buy in order to make the mast. The various sections will slide into one another. When you build these sections you can fit everything inside the boat when trailering it around so nothing hangs out. Another mast option is to buy one 20-foot piece of pipe and roll the sail up in it.

The 3-meter tri comes in 2 versions – a Constant Camber version and a Seaclipper version. The plywood Seaclipper version is actually a little faster.

We used to take 3-meter tris out racing at Lake Union, which is a closed fresh-water lake not far from downtown Seattle. Lake

Union is only about a mile long and a half-mile wide. We'd set up a little course with buoys and anchored boats so we could race. On one occasion, we used a boat anchored up at one end of the lake for a mark. (Keep in mind that most of the racers were adult middle-aged guys like me).

So there we were … racing around this lake in these 3-meter tris … and we were having a great time. As a bunch of us were going around that one mark at the end of the lake, there was a man and woman sitting on the boat watching us. All of a sudden, the guy sailing behind me started laughing uncontrollably. After our race he told me the guy had stood up and shouted, "*Look Martha, there are GROWNUPS in those boats!*"

To top it all off we were sailing in *wintertime*. You can sit down inside these little boats and your shoulders are at about deck level. We wore big puffy jackets and stayed nice and toasty in our little boats with thermoses full of hot toddy – or something else to keep our insides warm all day long. We could go out there and sail the little tris and it would practically be snowing. But we'd just sit inside the boats all warm and cozy and couldn't have cared less. We had a great time with those things.

There is an old saying that goes, "*The amount of fun you have in a boat is inversely proportional to its length!*" It just so happens that it's true when it comes to the 3-meter tris.

"The Constant Camber Boat Building System"

The Constant Camber boat building system was Jim Brown's invention. He actually had a patent for it at one time. We paid him royalties in order to use it.

It was developed because it can take a long time to finish off all of the hull surface area on multihull sides (6 sides on a trimaran and 4 on a catamaran) when building them conventionally. The conventional way of doing it involves setting up a bunch of frames and then covering those with a whole bunch of stringers. Afterwards, many strips of plywood are applied on top, while being angled forward and angled aft. Those are overlaid and glued to each other, which is a very labor-intense process. Lots of people trying to build bigger boats just flamed out using this process. It was just too much work.

The Constant Camber system is a cold molding technique in which we attempt to build boats much faster. But another benefit is that when you look at the hulls, you can't figure out if the material is wood or fiberglass. Boats constructed in Constant Camber have a very smooth contour to them. We've been able to build boats with very slender hulls using this technique, which includes small monohulls and rowing dinghies.

On the other hand, we've built catamarans up to 64 feet in length with Constant Camber. One 64-foot cat was certified to carry 149 passengers. We regard this system as *current* because it's still great for building boats with today. As a matter of fact, we've got a big catamaran being built in Oregon by Schooner Creek Boatworks. They're using the Constant Camber system to construct it. It's a $2,000,000 boat and will be certified to carry 90 passengers.

The Constant Camber system utilizes sheets of plywood or veneers laid across a mold. By the time an entire hull side is finished, it's all in one piece. And it possesses cross-wise curvature and length-wise curvature. The sides are built in almost exactly the shape they need, resulting in 2 peapod-like halves put together to complete the hull.

There was a cover on *Multihulls Magazine* once that showed a picture taken from inside the ama of a Norman Cross trimaran. The picture looked through all of the interior frames from aft forward. All you could see were frames inside this hull about every 2-3 feet, with little stringers about every 4-5 inches going all the way down this thing.

There were so many parts and pieces of wood that it looked like the inside of an aircraft. The picture also showed the boat's skin of plywood overlaid on top of the frames and stringers in order to complete the hull. Anybody who looked at that picture could see it must have taken a lot of work to build that boat. I thought to myself, "*Man, that picture is going to sell the Constant Camber system – no problem!*"

Constant Camber hulls under construction

More Small Trimarans

The reason the Constant Camber system works is because it enables a builder to create hulls without having to do unnecessary stuff. Both Jim and I thought we needed to get into cold molding boats because so much domestic marine plywood is of poor quality and imported ply is expensive. We need to be using material that is less expensive and then laminating it up ourselves, especially since we can use epoxy. This will create a much better product. So that concept eventually became this "inside-out" molding system.

We mold the skin of the boat first and then put the bulkheads in afterwards. A Constant Camber boat, as opposed to a conventionally built boat that uses frames, stringers and plywood overtop, results in about a 60% reduction in the number of parts. There is less material required to build a Constant Camber boat and you end up with basically the same boat you could have built conventionally.

Building with Constant Camber allows you to do away with at least half of the frames. Take my design known as the *CC Cyclone 23*, which is built using the Constant Camber method. It only has 2 frames in the boat, located at the point of the crossbeams (akas). There are no other frames inside the boat. And it's the same thing in the amas. A sailboat that size normally uses about 7 or 8 frames in construction. So that boat only uses about 20% of the frames normally found in a trimaran of similar size.

The less material used the more a builder saves on cost. The challenging thing about Constant Camber though is mental. It's a different paradigm than some builders are able to conceive. When describing it as a construction method, it's different from what most boat builders have ever conceived of.

A guy who builds a boat out of plywood using conventional plans is going to get his plans in the mail, figure out his material list, then go buy some material to get started building the frames that same day.

The Constant Camber approach is different. The first thing you do when constructing a Constant Camber boat is build a

An Interview with John Marples

laminating form or mold. Then you buy a bunch of laminating stock. This is often thin plywood or veneer because these materials are cheaper than other types of wood. We buy veneer when we can get it. Then you get some epoxy and you're ready. You start building hull pieces individually and before long you've got an entire hull completed.

Using Constant Camber works especially well when it comes to building a multihull. If you're just building a monohull then it may not make that much economic sense to build in Constant Camber. But if, for instance, you're building a catamaran with 4 hull sides, then Constant Camber now starts making more sense. With 6 hull sides, a trimaran can be an ideal boat to build using this system. Boats with more surface area are better for building in Constant Camber, which is especially true of multihulls.

When you first start using a Constant Camber mold you discover that you can knock out boat sections very quickly. The mold itself features an arc of a circle or accelerating curve. One side is slightly different than another. But the lengthwise curvature of this mold is a perfect radius. And that is the secret. Once you've established a pair of planks that go across the mold and have a reasonably good fit with each other, then you can start knocking out panel sections in a mass production format.

You could, for example, have stock for a panel that is 6 feet wide and 20 feet long and laminate it in about an hour. You'll just lay your first planks across the mold dry, then apply some epoxy on top, and then put the next layer down on top of it – with the angle going in the opposite direction. The planks you'll be handling are dry. Then you'll use vacuum pressure to squeeze everything together until it cures.

This process is so fast that even when I was doing lamination in my shop by myself, I'd be able to do 4 or 5 layers within the working time of even the fastest epoxy hardener. When the panel is ready to cure, you put a bag over it and attach the bag to a vacuum pump until the glue is hardened. When it's hard (a few hours later) you turn the vacuum pump off. The next morning you can pull the dried finished panel off the mold and start building another panel on the mold.

CC 26 FOLDING TRIMARAN UNDER CONSTRUCTION

MAIN HULL PANELS MATED OVER FORMERS

MAIN HULL PANELS SPLICED, READY FOR SANDING.

FORMER SET-UP. ACTUAL BULKHEAD WITHOUT LUMBER AND CUTOUTS.

An Interview with John Marples

I've done layups of full-sized sheets of plywood on a mold, edge-to-edge, in order to build panel sections 64 feet long. We had 5 guys building panels at one time and doing 3 layers during the process. It only took 2 hours per panel. So the Constant Camber system becomes even that much more efficient when building larger boats. Of course, panels like that are big. The 64-foot panels weighed 1300 lbs. apiece. But they had incredible strength because they had compound curvature to them ... like an eggshell.

Panel sections made with the Constant Camber system are not tender. In fact, one of the things gained by using Constant Camber is being able to shift some of the structural requirement usually associated with frames and stringers into the skin. The skin becomes a little bit heavier.

For instance, a 40-foot boat that has ½-inch skin built using Constant Camber need only have frames inside it about every 5 or 6 feet apart. But a conventionally built boat with a 3/8-inch skin will need lots of stringers and frames inside for support.

The damage resistance on the outside of both boats is also going to be different. The ½-inch Constant Camber skin is going to be much tougher – almost twice the penetration resistance to damage as the 3/8-inch plywood on the standard frame boat. And the compound curvature of the Constant Camber skin is also going to be much more resistant to hydrostatic pressures. A regular piece of plywood is always going to want to oilcan and turn inside out because it was always flat. So the compound curvature can make the hull structure so stiff and strong it sometimes seems incredible.

My 3-meter tri prototype was built out of 3 layers of 1/16-inch western-red-cedar veneers using the Constant Camber system. The main hull, fully glassed up, with the 2 panels together, only weighed 10 pounds. It was *very* lightweight. At boat shows, I'd tell people to go over to an ama and put their finger in the middle of it and push as hard as they could in order to see if they could see any deflection. They couldn't, even though the hull was only as thick as a piece of corrugated cardboard.

There were only 2 frames in that boat ... one at each aka. The 2 side hull pieces had simply been made on the Constant Camber mold and then glued together. The hull looked as if it had come out of a fiberglass mold -- except it was wood. Wood is a wonderful engineering material if used correctly.

The thinnest plywood available is about 1/8-of-an-inch thick (3 mm). That thickness is enough to build a 25 foot boat in Constant Camber. So any boat below 25 feet or so must really be built out of veneer using this system. You can use veneer pieces that are just 1/16, or even 1/20-of-an-inch thick.

This can become a difficulty, however, when building some smaller boats using Constant Camber because the radius of the mold that you have to bend the pieces around becomes fairly severe. You can't really bend 1/8-inch veneer around a sharp radius like that. Even if you could, you still need a minimum of 3 laminations to get the hull side stiff. So for smaller boats we used "style covers" from a door manufacturer as panel material.

These style covers were basically the external portions on the stain-quality doors you find at places like Lowes or Home Depot. If you can find a door manufacturer that uses this door cover material then you can try and go to their supplier and buy "seconds" of it. They'll be cheap and they can be used even if they're slightly damaged. Veneer door covers usually come about 7 feet long and 5 1/2 inches wide. We could usually get them in pine, fir, cedar or some other species. The challenge for us here in the U.S. market today, of course, is that many of those doors aren't made in the U.S. anymore. So this great building material may not be readily available to North American home boat builders.

On a positive note, we *do* have an almost endless supply of 1/8-inch lauan (close to 3 mm thick), often referred to as "doorskin" plywood, here in North America. You can get this a number of places, including many hardware stores and local lumberyards. The only caveat is that it should be tested to make sure that it's composed of waterproof glue.

This material is normally under 10 bucks a sheet and can be a nice quality product, depending upon where it comes from. Much of it comes from Indonesia. But I've heard recently that they don't ship any of it with interior glue anymore. If it were used on outside doors then it would peel apart after a short time of being outside. They're supposedly all made with waterproof glue nowadays. But don't believe it until you test the lauan first.

Take a sample piece from the lot you intend to buy from and perform the Gougeon Brothers test. Boil it for an hour in water, then dry it out in the toaster oven, then boil it in water again for an hour, then put it back into the toaster oven. If it survives that process then it's probably composed of waterproof glue.

We've had some certified boats that were built using this material in the past. So it works great for boat building in Constant Camber. As a matter of fact, in the *Gougeon Brothers on Boat Construction* book, they wrote about this material and how to use it because it's been used to build Tornado hulls and other things. You can use material like this and it doesn't have to be fancy, expensive stuff. Some of the material you can get out of your local lumberyard might be very adequate for a boat when using the Constant Camber system. It just depends upon the supplier.

It's not bad for $10 a sheet and I've used a lot of it. I've built 3-meter tris with it and lots of other boats too. You can also laminate over lauan with a core material and get a boat that is extremely light. The Gougeon brothers were laminating it over honeycomb craft paper and making incredibly lightweight structures from it. They made structures that were the equivalent of ½-inch plywood, yet weighed about ¼ of its weight.

The whole Constant Camber process is fascinating. As I mentioned before, I've put together boats that were 64 feet long with 1-inch-thick panels. And I've put boats together that were 10 feet long with just 3/16 inch panels and the process is exactly the same. In fact, my proof of concept for a particular hull is often to build a model in my shop here using a model Constant Camber mold.

"The Constant Camber Cyclone 23"

The Cyclone 23 was designed as a daysailer for taking spins around the bay on sunny afternoons. It could also be used for extensive camping and cruising. I built the first one for myself as a "proof of concept" boat.

I'd always envisioned buying a pup tent, or one with fiberglass bows large enough to cover the entire cockpit. Then the bottom could be cut out in order to create an enclosure that snaps onto the hull around the cockpit area. That would give a camper a great soft cabin to protect them from mosquitoes and rain. It would be a very cheap way to go cruising.

I actually thought about this when designing the boat. It's one reason why the tiller comes through the bulkhead at the end of the cockpit instead of over the top. This would allow the builder to have an uninterrupted tent over the cockpit without any problem.

The Cyclone 23 is a really fun boat. It's got a 3-wire rig that can be adapted from beach cats. There are a number of beach cats that you could use rigging from to power the boat. I also designed a dedicated rig for it if the builder wants. The forward stay is set up like a screecher, meaning that the stay itself revolves in bearings so you can have a roller furler on the jib. When the boat is trailered, the rolled up jib can just be coiled up and put into the cockpit because it doesn't have a stiff foil extrusion.

The mast raising system for the CC 23 is designed into the trailer, whose plans are included along with the plans to build the sailboat. The idea is to help owners raise the rig so they can go sailing rather quickly.

My definition of a "trailerable" boat is one that sails away from the dock within an hour of you arriving at the launch ramp with it behind your car. The first time you set up the boat will probably take about 2 or 3 hours. But after you get the hang of it and how to do the things that need to be done quickly, then the entire process can be done within an hour. This means if you want to go sailing for the day (and I've done this) you can pull the boat out of the driveway that morning, go down to the water, go sailing, then come back to the dock, put the boat on the trailer and go home that night.

"Cyclone" 23 trimaran

The CC 23 doesn't have quite as slick of a folding system as the CC 26 does. It takes a little bit longer to bolt things up. But it's still fairly easy. Its folding system is useable only on the ground, meaning that the boat is launched "full width." It's unfolded on the trailer before going into the water. (It folds out to 17 feet wide).

More Small Trimarans

It's not like a Farrier, where you slide the boat into the water and then unfold the boat as you're getting ready to sail out of the harbor. That's nice to be able to do, of course. But those types of folding systems are complex, very heavy and very expensive. I didn't want to burden my builders with that kind of weight or expense. Mine is a very simple linkage.

The whole construction process of the boat is very simple too. There is nothing very complex. There is considerable savings in the parts count compared with a boat that is built the conventional plywood way. In fact, I've had a number of people come back to me and say, "*Oh man, I'd really love to build that 23' boat, but I just don't want to build it in Constant Camber. I want to do it in plywood.*" What they don't realize is that building it in plywood would be a lot more work.

The Constant Camber system is so abbreviated and slick that it's incredible. The mold for this boat is about 4 1/2 feet wide and about 14 feet long. It fits in a one-car garage with no problem. You set up the mold, and then build half-length panels for each hull side.

After the panels are finished on the mold, they're stitched and glued together. Then you put fiberglass cloth over the joints on the inside and outside of the hulls. There are easy ways to do this too, which I share with builders who order a set of plans. What you end up with is a beautiful fiberglass taping with no bubbles and all the glass is neatly faired out so you don't have to touch it anymore. You're done with it. If you do this process correctly there is no need for sanding and no messing around with the hull panels afterwards. The boat is ready for paint once you get done with the glassing. You can save yourself a lot of effort this way. It's wonderful!

One thing we noticed about conventional plywood building is that it takes so much time to complete the fairing process. Constant Camber fixes this problem. The conventional methods, which include putting up frames and stringers with double diagonal planking on them, end up creating a surface that isn't very smooth. This means things have to be sanded down and then fairing compound needs to be applied. Then things are sanded down again and the process goes on. It can go on for what seems like forever. Builders eventually arrive at a point where the appearance of the exterior of the hulls is acceptable to them.

More Small Trimarans

That whole routine can be avoided by using the Constant Camber system. It's fairly simple to do. And the panels you end up with after taking them off the mold are extremely smooth. In fact, I've *never* had to do any fairing on a Constant Camber panel!

An Interview with John Marples

When building in Constant Camber, the hull sides come off of the mold so smooth that you really don't need to touch them at all most of the time. If there are any dried epoxy drops anywhere then they can be taken off with a sander in minutes. Apart from that, any sanding you do would probably actually damage the fairness already existing on the panels.

You can also do most of the glass and finishing work on the panels without having to do it vertically. You can set up sawhorses to hold all your panels in place while working on one side at a time – both outside and inside. It's so easy to work this way because the hull panels are all laid out nice and flat in front of you. All you have to do is leave a bare strip of wood along the panel edges at the points where they're going to be joined with other panel sections.

The reduction in materials and labor can be pretty significant when building a boat using the Constant Camber system. It also means you can build that boat much faster than in traditional plywood. As soon as your mold is constructed you can start building your hull panels. When you need to join the panels together you can use your mold for that too because it lets your panels keep their lengthwise curvature. You can line the panels up so that one panel isn't skewed in relationship to the other one.

The most challenging part a builder is going to have to deal with when building a Constant Camber boat is paying attention to the fiberglass taping that will have to be done on the joint up at the bow. There can be a buildup of thickness there when the 2 hull halves come together. That may require a little bit of fairing on the hull side to smooth out the taped joint. But that's about it.

I include a booklet with the boat plans called *Liquid Joinery*, which describes the materials and processes used for joining the wooden panels together when they're ready. It contains recipes and pictures for mixing various epoxy applications and fillers. It also has samples that can be used to make plastic squeegees for applying epoxy on various joint radiuses on hull forms. You can even pre-cut various squeegees so the right one is always available when you need it.

The finished panels have a compound curve that is very rigid, meaning that even when you push the bulkhead frames down inside the hulls you can't make the skin bulge around the frame positions. That is something guys using the cylinder molding method have to wrestle with all the time. In essence, they're forcing the shape of the boat by pushing the bulkheads down into the skin. It can end up with a hull looking like a carthorse that has been starved. Sometimes the builders are able to see every "bone" in the side of their boat.

"Low Drama Amas"

The Cyclone 23 can accommodate 6 people in the cockpit very comfortably. The cockpit seats are 8 feet long. So there is a full sheet length of plywood between the 2 crossbeams. There is a ton of room inside the cockpit. There is enough room for 6 people to sit down and nobody has to move when making the boat "come about." I often had 6 people in my Cyclone 23 for daysails and everyone had plenty of room.

The first portion of the cockpit is covered over with a tiny cuddy cabin. The reason for that is when you're sailing fast, some spray is probably going to get the cockpit a little wet eventually. So I designed a storage place for coats, cameras and regular gear so those things can stay dry.

This cuddy area forward in the hull really isn't a place for adults, although kids can crawl around in there. The cockpit seats are wide enough to sleep on for camp-cruising. If you wanted something wider than that then you could put something between the seats that would create room enough for a huge bed area.

There is a little sheet winch on top of the cuddy cabin, which goes to both jib sheets. The mainsheet is on a traveler at the back end of the cockpit and the tiller comes into the cockpit back there also. And there is room enough to fit a cooler in the cockpit if you want to take one along.

The boom is located well above everyone's head so nobody has to duck when they're sitting down. I'm 6' 4" inches tall and I never had to duck my head when sitting down inside the cockpit.

When I built the 26-footer, I constructed it so that its amas would just barely touch the water. Most of the time, one ama was in the water and one was out. This was great for sailing in light airs and overall performance of the boat. But when somebody stepped off a dock onto the boat, the ama they stepped onto sunk down to accept their weight. So the boat tended to be very lively. Some people didn't like that.

So I thought about this when designing the 23-footer. I knew its owners were going to want to take lots of friends out sailing and they probably weren't going to be familiar with multihulls. So I gave the floats quite a bit of initial immersion. I call them the "*low-drama amas*." This means people can step aboard the Cyclone 23 and it doesn't move much because it already has enough displacement on the ama to allow it to hold a person's weight. It won't flop around at the dock. So the ama design offers more stability when boarding and leaving the boat.

I used to leave my 23-footer down at the local harbor so I could go out for an hour or two of daysailing whenever I'd occasionally have some time during an afternoon. It was great for taking a spin around the bay. I'd untie the boat when I got down to the dock, jump onto it, throw the dock lines in the nets, walk into the cockpit, pull the roller furler string loose from the cam cleat, unfurl the jib and then grab onto the tiller and sail out of the harbor. (I could sail out of the harbor on the jib alone). Then I'd point the boat into the wind, get the mainsail out and hooked up, then pull it up and go sailing. Coming back in, I'd do the reverse. It was *so* easy.

There is a long telescoping extension on the tiller of this sailboat. It allows you to stand on the ama deck and steer the boat if you want to. Or you can sit in the cockpit with one hand on the tiller and the other hand on engine controls if you ever need to. The engine is on a plank that sticks out from the hull's side. But it's located in such a way that when you're sitting on that side in the cockpit seat, you can reach over and touch the engine's power head and throttle control. When you start sailing you can then tilt the engine up so it's out of the water. So everything is designed for convenient sailing.

There is not much need to venture out onto the amas unless you want to. If you have the spinnaker up and you need to readjust the sheets to an outboard location then you'd need to hike out a bit. But otherwise, you can stay right in the cockpit when sailing.

I used to sail around Puget Sound in my CC 23 and one of the places where we'd go had great big ferries going into the town across the bay. Those ferries would sometimes truck along at 20+ knots. They didn't create much of a bow wave but they did leave a great big wake. When I'd be out sailing by myself, I'd be able to get the boat up to about 10-12 knots and hit an edge of one of these wakes. The boat would almost fly out of the water before landing on the next wave crest. I thought, *"Wow, this is fun!"*

One day I got my wife to go sailing with me and told her, *"You've got to come out and experience this ... it's so much fun!"* She consented and we went out on the 23-foot trimaran to meet the ferry. I sailed up to its wake, and just before our take-off, realized there wasn't quite as much wind as those times before. My boat was only going about 8 knots. In addition, the boat was now carrying the weight of an added passenger. Too late. The boat went off the edge of the wake and ... well ... the boat didn't quite fly out so high, or as far. I stuffed its bow into the next wave. *Swoosh.* There was a big crash of rushing water that swept all over us. *"Ooooooh Dear ... I'm soooooo sorry!"* I shouted to my wife. I have to laugh when thinking about it now. I'd never got wet before. But that time was different.

"A Piece Of Cake To Sail"

The Cyclone 23 is a piece of cake to sail. It's very stable. If you put the full-sized rig on the boat, which includes the 31-foot mast designed for it, with a good mainsail and jib, then the boat will probably sail at wind speed most of the time. I probably had the boat up to about 16 knots on occasion, which is really flying along in a boat that size. And I could always sail with just 2 fingers on the tiller to make it steer. You can do zigzags in the waves if you want without any effort at all. It was always a well-mannered boat.

You can run this boat right up onto the beach if you want too. The rudder and centerboard both "kick-up." The boat only draws about a foot and a half of water. So it's great for shallow areas. The whole boat is light enough that you can just push off a bar or beach if you run aground. The whole boat is only going to weigh about 1200 lbs when fully assembled.

The roller furler jib is great because everything is in reach when you need to change a sail. You don't have to fool around with hanks or anything ... just roll it out and roll it back in again when you're done with it. And you can launch the spinnaker from the cockpit. The J-24 spinnaker, which was designed for keelboats, works very well with the Cyclone 23. There should be lots of inexpensive used ones available.

The most expensive part of the rigging will be the 6-part mainsheet block from Harken (http://www.harken.com). They can sometimes be a little pricey but this part is well worth the expense. Making the mainsheet easy to pull in goes a long way in improving comfort inside the boat.

This sailboat also features a storage hatch on the aft deck. You can reach into it from the cockpit to put the motor in and lock it away so it doesn't get stolen. The fuel for the motor can also be kept inside this back hatch within a portable gas tank.

You only need a 4 –to-6 horsepower outboard motor for this boat. So it'll be very light.

The steering, of course, comes via the tiller that is attached at the end of the cockpit. It has 2 lines that go up to a crank on the rudder. You can pop up the rudder just a little bit if you need to reduce draft. And then you can pop it all the way up when you need to. The whole kick-up system on this boat works pretty well.

"This Can Save a Homebuilder Tons of Money"

I wrote a booklet entitled, *Panel Making* that describes the Constant Camber system. It's a generic instruction manual for building all Constant Camber panels, regardless of what Constant Camber model you're building – including the mold. It covers sources for materials too.

Then there is the booklet called, *Liquid Joinery* that covers how to use epoxy. (Jim Brown wrote part of it and I wrote part of it). Then I have another booklet called *Standard Details*, which is a bunch of cartoons showing readers how to build multiple things. For example, one cartoon shows you how to build wooden cleats. And I provide various sizes of cleats and their dimensions and so forth.

I often tell guys who like to build boat parts at home to find some old wooden pallets that are made with oak rails. Take the rails off and use a bandsaw to make cleats with that oak wood. The oak is hard as a rock and is very strong. Shiny factory-made cleats at a shop can cost around $15 apiece. There are also cartoons inside it that show how to build your own blocks and anchors and all sorts of stuff. So doing this can save a homebuilder tons of money when constructing their own boat.

I send these booklets out with the plans when a homebuilder orders them. None of my boats come with a set of instructions on where to begin and where to finish. But my plans are often in a pictorial format. They offer perspective drawings that show various parts of the building process. Even people that have never built anything from plans before usually have no problem building the boats. My phone doesn't ring that much from plan buyers who need to ask lots of questions. Most builders have no problem reading the plans or understanding what I'm trying to tell them in the drawings.

There are quite a few sheets of drawings for the Cyclone 23. I'm currently building an airplane that has fewer drawings in its plans than are in my boat plans for the Cyclone 23. I like drawing plans. I sit at the drawing table and build the boat in my mind using the set of plans that I'm creating. So I keep asking myself, *"What information do I need in order to build this part and put this thing together with that piece?"* And so on.

I keep on adding drawings until I think I've got the essence of the process down on paper. Occasionally I have to revise things as time goes on. But in general, my customers tend to like my plans.

I used to have a "plans agent," who was a fellow that once worked for Glen-L (http://www.glen-l.com) until finally going into business for himself. He designed all kinds of boats and used to sell his plans through magazines and on the Internet. I sent him a set of Cyclone 23 plans to look over one day. He called me up and said, *"John, those are the most beautiful plans I've ever seen in my life."* I thought that was quite a compliment coming from him.

This brings up another point though. When a customer buys a set of plans from me they can always contact me if they don't understand something in the plans. There are some designers out there who will sell a set of plans and then suddenly become "unavailable" to customers who have a question afterwards. In my opinion, a part of the designer's job is to also be available *after* somebody purchases a set of their plans.

There is even a drawing in the CC 23 plans that shows it on a trailer with the mast being raised. In order to get the mast up on this boat you need some power. You've got to do it properly with block and tackle because you don't want to lose control as it's being raised. So my drawing shows exactly how to do this without any difficulty. It's fairly simple. But you have to do things properly.

I even include the sheet entitled, *Trailer Plans* with the Cyclone 23 package. You can build a boat trailer a number of different ways. I've built lots of trailers. The way I normally build them is to set up 2 main supports crossed with 2 bulkhead supports going across those. Then you can insert a couple of frame rails. This can all be done using either wood or steel. My plans show how to build a trailer frame entirely out of steel or entirely out of wood or using a combination of the two materials. This booklet also includes an inexpensive list of suppliers for everything needed – including things like axles and springs.

A sailor can go out and buy a trailer if they don't want to make one. Then they can fit it out with the proper supports necessary to carry this particular sailboat model. I regard the trailer as a part of the whole design because it's a required part of making the whole boat-user-process work. If you're going to trailer your boat then you need a trailer that is properly designed for your boat to fit on to get it to the water and back home again.

Commercial parts and fittings and so forth can be *very* expensive. I picked up a catalogue the other day and looked at the prices for some small fittings that I was thinking of buying and I was shocked at how expensive they were. So constructing the Cyclone 23, including its trailer and fittings, is going to be a very cost effective way for a sailor to acquire a high performance small trimaran. If you're willing to put in a little sweat equity then you can build one of my boats for far less than any of the commercial ones on the market.

....

For more about the *Cyclone 23 Trimaran*, and all of John Marples' other designs, visit **http://www.searunner.com/ ...**

Information continues on next page ...

More Small Trimarans

John Marples' booklets (*Liquid Joinery, Panel Making & Standard Details*), mentioned in this chapter, are available for sale individually at his website.
Contact information for John Marples can be found at this website.

Chapter 17

An Interview with Jim Brown

Designer of the Searunner Trimarans, & New "Seaclipper 20"

I lived in Miami, Florida during the early 1950s. After graduating from high school I briefly attended an Ivy League university but ended up in Florida as a young man searching for some direction in life.

While living there, I joined a scuba diving club in my early 20s. One of the guys in the club had a sister who was the girlfriend of a man named Mike Burke. Mike was about to become the founder of a Miami business called *Windjammer Barefoot Cruises*. Mike planned to acquire large vessels on which he could host scuba diving parties or "clubs," as he referred to them.

I was on board Mike's schooner when his club chartered it to the Bahamas for a long weekend of diving. But I found myself fascinated with the ship rather than the diving. When we got back to Miami I said to Mike, "*Let me come and work for you. I only need enough money for food, lodging and some laundry money.*" So I went to work for him and became one of his first employees.

Mike soon acquired a 150-foot Windjammer schooner. It carried diving charters of up to 20 people at a time on 10-day excursions from Miami to the Bahamas and Cuba and also the Yucatan. There was a fellow in Mike's crew named Fred McKenzie, who taught me the ways of the Windjammer. He eventually helped me become a mate on this sailing schooner.

Up to the point of working on that schooner I'd only done a little bit of sailing. But then I really became fascinated with it.

I worked on the schooner for about a year. During that time there was another guy who started working on the crew named Wolfgang Kraker. Wolfgang was my age but had crossed the Atlantic from Holland in his own boat -- a welded sheet metal catamaran.

Seeing Wolf's boat was my first introduction to multihulls. I never went sailing in it though. I found it "indescribably offensive." The notion of it having 2 hulls just didn't seem right to me at the time. I couldn't understand how this guy had crossed the Atlantic in that boat.

Both Wolfgang and I later joined another crew and did quite a bit of sailing together. After a series of events, we eventually managed to get ourselves marooned on the Caribbean side of Columbia in South America. While there, we built a trimaran out of oil drums and somehow managed to sail that thing to Panama. From there we were able to get back to Miami.

As you can see, my introduction to multihulls was extremely crude. To be honest, I wasn't satisfied with those multihull vessels at all. But I was quite amazed at the rock bottom cost one could be built for.

After getting back to the States I decided I needed to have a boat of my own. My path led me to wanting to know how to build boats in fiberglass, which was a relatively new material back then. There were really no large products being built in the US with fiberglass yet (this was probably about 1957).

"A Man Named Arthur Piver"

I went to San Francisco because I heard about a company that was building a traditional 40-foot sloop in fiberglass. I applied for a job and got hired by them (the Coleman Boat and Plastics Company). This company was in Sausalito, California and it turned out they were real pioneers when it came to building boats in fiberglass.

I was having a great time back then. I lived on a houseboat, drove around on a motorcycle and worked at Coleman's. The Sausalito waterfront was quite a place to live in those years. It was at the beginning stage of what eventually became the Sausalito houseboat community.

After a period of time, however, I began to feel "boatless." It was about this time that I happened to meet with a man named Arthur Piver.

Arthur lived in the next town over, a place called Mill Valley. He was experimenting with his first trimarans on Richardson's Bay, which is an arm of San Francisco Bay. I saw him go by in one of his boats one day and was completely captivated by it. I managed to find him and he took me out sailing in his boat.

I essentially became a Piver protégé. I began to see the inherent excellent sea-keeping properties of the modern "double outrigger canoe."

I sailed Piver's little 16-footer with him, a boat he called *Frolic*, which was little more than a collection of plywood boxes. We took this boat out to the Golden Gate and back again thru incredible conditions. We surfed the wakes of freighters coming back in towards the shore and I began to realize the enormous potential of multihulls.

There was always, of course, the inherent danger of capsize. And those early Piver boats suffered from things like rudder failures, centerboard failures and de-mastings. But his boats were always strong enough and they never came apart even though we frequently took them into conditions where you wouldn't take other little boats. There is a roaring tide in the water out by the Golden Gate. And day in and day out, San Francisco has some of the strongest winds of any sailing center in the world. So we tested those early trimarans in extreme conditions.

After sailing with Arthur Piver for a period of time, the Coleman Company began bouncing paychecks off its workers. So I went to work building houses in the High Sierras. I stayed there until I realized one winter that being up to my waist in snow while working wasn't what I really wanted to do.

I began thinking about going back to the Caribbean. So I went back to San Francisco and approached Arthur Piver about extending the length of his 16-foot boat Frolic by adding another sheet of plywood, which would make it 24 feet long. The jump in size seemed huge to me at the time. But it turned out Piver had already drawn out plans for such a vessel and a man in San Francisco had already constructed it.

This bigger trimaran was designed as a 4-passenger open daysailer. The guy who built it offered to take me out for a ride. We went out to the Gate and then came back. I was convinced this boat could make a long coastal voyage. The boat was so small and light that if a sailor faced strong storm conditions the boat could just be sailed right up onto a beach. I began looking at this boat design as a way to get myself back down to the Caribbean. So I started building this new Piver design, which he referred to as the *Nugget*.

The Nugget was originally intended to be an open boat. Even today, I regard the Piver Nugget as the most inherently perfect boat Arthur Piver ever designed. At least it was until he responded to pressure from customers who wanted to take the centerboards out in order to put a big cabin on it. His original design featured a deep centerboard and a deep rudder. There was no super-structure on the original design either. In my opinion, the design changes Arthur later made to the Nugget only degraded the vessel.

For the coastal trip I planned on making, I did need a little cuddy cabin. So I built a tiny one on my boat. But it wasn't any bigger than the little bonnet on a VW Beetle.

I had started building my Nugget in Sausalito around 1958. By the time I'd finished it I was married. My wife Joanna and I were also expecting our first child. And you know what? It's funny to think about it now, but I thought we'd try and sail to the Caribbean anyway. We sailed out past the Golden Gate one day and turned left, heading south … with my wife 5 ½ months pregnant.

We headed to Panama to cross the Isthmus … or so I thought! We never made it, of course. We had a few adventures along the way and ended up bringing the boat back to Sausalito on land through Mexico. But having taken that coastal voyage in a modern trimaran made me sort of an "instant expert."

When we arrived in Sausalito I went to work for Arthur Piver as an agent for his designs in order to help him sell plans. By that time he was working on a 30-foot design he called the "*Nimble*." Arthur eventually went on to cross the Atlantic Ocean in the Nimble. He trailered it in pieces to New York, where he launched the boat in 1961 for an ocean crossing.

By the early 1960s, Hawaiian-type catamarans had already done some ocean crossings. The design of Woody Brown and Rudy Choy had already humiliated the Corinthian community with its performance in the Pacific. And James Wharram had already crossed the Atlantic in 1956. So things were rolling along in the world of multihulls. But Arthur Piver was a gifted copywriter and was a great promoter, which made most of the enthusiasm for multihulls centered on trimarans for a while … particularly in California.

There were certain structural disadvantages catamarans faced at the time that weren't an issue for trimarans. There was really no place to step the mast on cats, no place to mount the centerboard, no place to mount a single rudder and no place to attach the head stay. All of these factors made the mid 20th century trimarans, such as Arthur Piver's, easier to design than catamarans.

In my opinion, the cultural atmosphere at the time had a lot to do with the emergence of the modern trimaran. The thousands of multihulls built in backyards during the '60s came about as a result of the combined "can-do spirit" and "escapism" during those years. A lot of multihull builders then had a sort of escapist-utopian frame of mind. They dreamed of sailing off into the sunset to find their own Shangri-La.

In the meantime, I was beginning to get big ideas about designing my own boats. A friend and I had starting building another Piver design -- a 40-foot trimaran called "*Victress*." I wanted to make some design changes on this boat though. My friend, who was financing this project, encouraged me to share my ideas with him. And it wasn't long afterwards that I hung out my own shingle as a "boat designer," much to the displeasure of Arthur Piver.

Arthur had a few key protégés from those years, myself included. We had all helped him develop and sail his early designs. And all of us, except one, eventually went into the business of designing our own boats. Piver deserves credit for stimulating the living daylights out of us. He was a wonderful guy out on the water. He was like a big kid when he was out sailing and his enthusiasm had been infectious.

"The Searunner 25"

The Searunner 25 was the smallest boat in the Searunner line of trimarans that I designed. And it was the only Searunner model under 30 feet long. The 25-footer was the 4th vessel in the line. It was also the smallest boat that I'd designed up to that time.

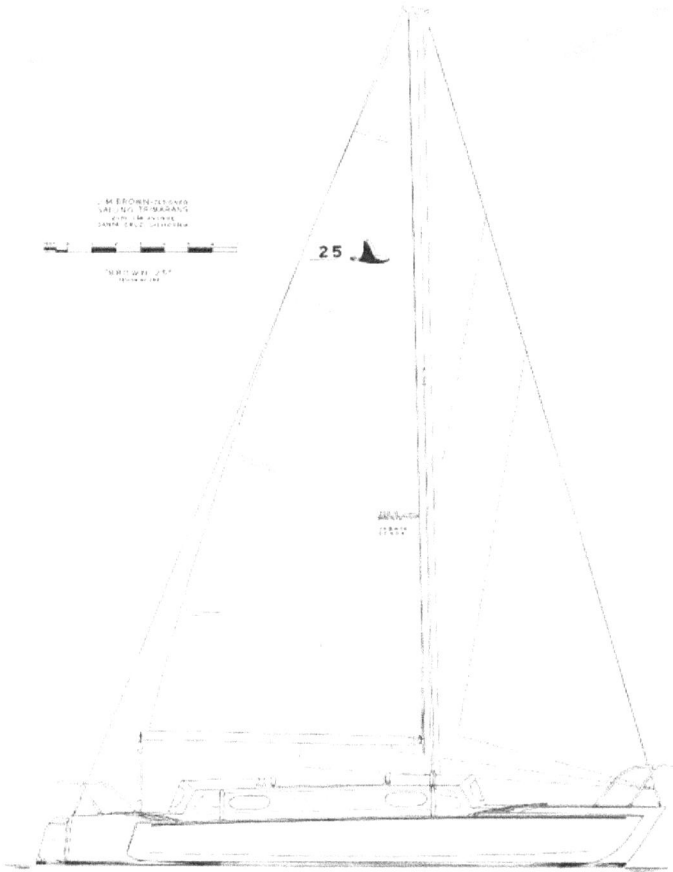

Searunner 25 - sketch #1

Even though it's only 25 feet long it was designed to be a true seafaring boat. I know of one 25-footer that crossed the Pacific, from California to Hawaii, and others completed ocean crossings too.

More Small Trimarans

There was a big structural change made in this boat from my 3 previous designs. I abandoned the notion of having to use 1-piece crossbeams. Up to this point, my trimarans were developed with single-piece box spars that went through the main hull and out to the floats. It turned out that – engineering wise, at least conceptually – it was easier to attach a beam and outriggers onto a trimaran's central hull than it was to bridge the hulls together, like on a catamaran.

We had learned that having big box spars passing through the main hull was a terrible interruption to interior accommodations inside cruisers. You often had to "duck under" them in order to get from one end of the interior to the other. And spar beams were also very heavy.

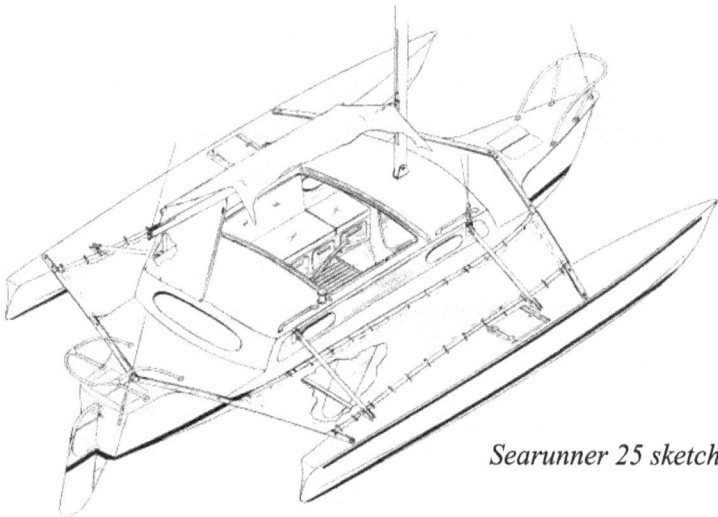

Searunner 25 sketch #2

I replaced the main crossbeams in the main hull of the Searunner 25 with what might be called a "diaphragm bulkhead," or a "main-strength" bulkhead, if you will. This idea wasn't the result of original thinking on my part. It had been done in aircraft for a long time, as well as in some other multihulls. It was essentially a sandwich bulkhead – plywood on both sides of a lumber truss.

View from the mast top of the Searunner 25

More Small Trimarans

It was possible to build this bulkhead in such a way that a big hole could be cut in the middle of it without interrupting its strength. So sailors could pass through the cutouts inside the main hull to get from one end of the boat to the other, without having to duck under beams. The bulkheads in the 25-footer extended outward only as far as the cabin side panels, which were 8 feet apart. This meant the cabin itself was only 8 feet wide and could be trailered.

Then I used what I referred to as the "A-frame outrigger beam," to make the Searunner into a trimaran, which was simply 2 aluminum pipes. One pipe was bonded to the float and the other pipe fastened onto the float in such a way that it articulated at the float deck.

On the other side, these pipes fastened onto metal pieces attached to the main strength bulkhead inside the main hull. The outriggers were attached to and detached from the main hull with pins. And pulling one of the pins out allowed each float to be folded downward. This may have been a primitive first version of today's popular trimaran folding systems.

It turned out the main hull had to be mounted up rather high in order to fit this folded trimaran onto a trailer. When the floats folded down they'd conflict with the fenders on a trailer unless the main hull was raised up in order to tuck the floats in alongside the main hull. So the Searunner 25 turned out not to be an ideal boat for trailering because a sailor needed quite a bit of deep water at a launching ramp. Most owners probably ended up taking the floats off when transporting their boat on a trailer.

A big advantage to having a Searunner 25 was that it could be built in one place and then launched at another. The fact it could be either trailered or demounted was ideal for that purpose.

Another benefit of using aluminum tube crossbeams for this design was that they could be driven through the waves without pounding them. That turned out to be very important when it came to sailing a very small seafaring boat such as this because of the weight issues encountered during a long trip.

It's easy to overload a multihull if making a long voyage. Sailing the 25-footer from California to Hawaii, for example, meant that a sailor would have to be very careful with their water supply. Since supplies for a longer trip add weight to a boat, especially water, the boat can become weighed down for long cruises. When driving a boat like this to windward, the float has to be driven through wave crests. Since these A-frame beams didn't pound in the waves they really helped this small boat be able to make long trips possible without the boat getting damaged.

Many solid-winged multihulls have a long history of suffering damage -- even modern ones. If you push a boat hard enough through waves and keep pounding it then it'll only be able to take so much before getting damaged. Overloading is a big reason why crossbeams get pounded on multihulls. So having thin crossbeams on this design really helped keep the boat structurally sound when out to sea.

All of the modern racers now feature their crossbeams in a gull-wing pattern. The idea is to keep the outboard portion of the beams up above the wave tops. They got that idea from Dick Newick, who taught the world how to go very fast in rough water. Streamlining crossbeams so they chop the top off waves offsets the pounding force against the boat.

"Long Distance Cruising"

The Searunner 25 was primarily designed for 1 or 2 people to do long distance cruising. Four people could certainly go daysailing in the boat. But it was great for single-hand long distance cruising.

My Searunner 25 design was an attempt to make a truly seafaring small trimaran. It offered good shelter. And it had an extremely well protected cockpit right in the center of the boat.

The cockpit sat on top of the centerboard trunk. Then it had a small front cabin forward of the cockpit and another small cabin aft of the cockpit. This boat also had something the Piver Nugget didn't have, which was a means to keep the sea from boarding her over the stern. By moving the cockpit into the middle of the boat and building a small super-structure around it, the cockpit was well protected and had a much better chance to avoid sailors getting "pitched out" of it in heavy weather.

Searunner 25 being trailered

Searunner 25 construction featured a unique way of building the chine. I devised a molded chine for the inside of the boat that utilized fiberglass tape in order to come up with a compound progressive bevel that didn't require expert carpentry skills. Of course, epoxy today would be even better. We called it a "molded chine" and it really worked well, even with just polyester resin. It allowed an amateur homebuilder to achieve a relatively sophisticated hull form. Those boats could take a pounding on that chine joint on the bottom of the hull without damage.

Another feature in the Searunner series, including the Searunner 25, was that ama/float hulls were asymmetric. The outboard side was slightly flatter than the inboard side. The only way to accomplish that was to have a chine. One chine was offset from the centerline farther than the other one.

Asymmetric hulls are classic. They probably go back about 2,000 years or more. A great many of the ancient multihulls featured asymmetric hulls. The first designer to use asymmetric hulls on his multihulls was Woody Brown in Hawaii. And he got the idea from actually looking at outrigger canoes in the Pacific Islands. Those were all single-outrigger proas. In order to keep their boats from sliding sideways they made the downwind side of the hulls flatter than the upwind sides.

The asymmetric hulls generate lift against the direction of the wind when the boat is under sail. They were used for years on modern catamarans. It worked well on catamarans before sailors started using deep daggerboards to keep their boats from sliding sideward instead.

While the Searunner 25 does feature a centerboard, I also designed it with asymmetric floats because they help keep smaller trimarans like this one from sliding sideways even more than they help catamarans. When going to windward, the weather hull is completely out of the water. The downwind float is being immersed. So the asymmetric float, together with the centerboard, is responsible for the general reputation that Searunners had for being very "weatherly" boats. They could climb to windward in very hard wind and leave most monohulls twice their size in the dust. A good part of the reason they could do that was because of those asymmetric floats.

When it comes to the performance of any boat, including the Searunner 25, so much depends upon a number of factors, including the condition of the sails and the abilities of the sailor. It's very difficult to talk about this without talking about specific variables.

More Small Trimarans

Most sailing takes place in about 10-15 knots of wind. In that kind of wind a Searunner could typically go about 7-8 knots. On a close reach, it may have gone about 10 knots. And when sailing close hauled to windward, in 15 knots of wind, the boat would make good at 7 knots with a leeway of less than 5 degrees. And sailing in 15-knot winds, with a 3-to-4 foot chop, the boat could sail 100 degrees between tacks. On flat water, it would go 85-90 degrees between tacks. When power reaching, in winds of 20-25 knots, the boat was capable of 12-15 knots with no problem. And when surf riding, of course, the boat might go close to 20 knots. This all, of course, assumes the boat had good sails and a good sailor. It's a very subjective estimation.

Multihull performance is also affected by how clean the hulls are on the bottom. Multis are very susceptible to "fouling." It can affect their performance more than monohulls because of their greater surface area.

The Searunner 25 was designed with a traditional Marconi masthead rig with a standing backstay. The shrouds went out only as far as the main hull cabin sides. So it was a single-spreader masthead rig, which was very common at the time. The arrangement of the original rig was to step the mast atop the forward main-strength bulkhead. Some builders put used mastheads on their Searunners.

Later on, after I began designing larger boats with diaphragm bulkheads, I rigged them as cutters. This meant the mast had to be moved some distance aft. A cutter rig carries 2 headsails so it needs a much larger "J-dimension," which means the distance from the mast out to the bow has to be somewhat larger for the cutter than with a sloop rig.

Pushing the cutter rig back on those multihulls was good because it pushed the weight back and got the drive farther back on the boat, which tended to reduce their tendency to have the bows pushed down when driving the boat hard. So later on, I started to offer the Searunner 25 with optional plans for a cutter rig.

An Interview with Jim Brown

I designed the cutter mast to be longer, and instead of stepping it on the cabin top, it was moved to go into the forward cabin on a stump that delivered the load down to the centerboard trunk. This transferred all of the strain from the bottom of the mast downward into the centerboard trunk. And that gave the colander load stress from the sail a wider area of distribution throughout the main hull.

This rig adjustment also gave sailors another advantage. It allowed the sails to be reefed from inside the cockpit. So one didn't have to go out on the deck to hoist, drop sails or reef. When this change took place I felt like I really had a "searunner." All of the larger Searunners have their masts stepped inside the cockpit. The greatest single danger sailors face is falling overboard. So this offered sailors a very big benefit.

All of the original Searunners were designed with wooden masts. A homebuilder could build their own box-spar mast if they wanted to. But the plans also included the specs for an aluminum mast.

My concept for the Searunner 25 was to design the smallest boat possible that would allow 2 people to sail offshore. By "offshore," I mean capable of handling extensive cruising. A few were cruised extensively. I know that sailors crossed both the Atlantic and Pacific in Searunner 25s.

The Searunner 25 was also attractive to people who wanted to have separate cabins for privacy. There was a single cabin aft and a single cabin up forward. That meant that when underway, with a 2-person crew, the off watch was able to sleep in peace. The person on watch could cook and navigate from inside the stern area.

"Wind Vane Self-Steering"

Sailors were able to climb into their own secure cabins to look at their charts and hear the radio and all of that. They steered the boat either from inside the cockpit or by using a wind-actuated self-steering device … also known as *wind-vane self-steering*! We put wind-vane steering on all the Searunners, including the 25-footer.

Searunner 25 under sail

There was a big club of model sailboat racers in London and wind-vane self-steering originated with their round pond racing sailboat models. These model boat enthusiasts wanted their boats to sail from one side of the pond to the other while keeping on the proper point of sail. So they devised a wind rudder, which was like a rudder sticking up in the air. It was bigger than the water rudder and it would sense the apparent wind. If the boat began to wander from its course then the wind rudder would sense the change in wind direction over the boat and talk (by way of a mechanical link) to the rudder on the boat, which turned the boat back on course.

You don't see a lot of wind vane self-steering anymore, except on very serious cruising boats, because everybody nowadays is into electric autopilots. But back then we didn't have autopilots. So we used these contraptions … stuck up in the wind. I think one of my greatest achievements was applying these self-steering wind vanes to my Searunners. I mean, there were probably hundreds of people that crossed oceans using those things without ever hardly touching the helm, even in storm conditions. A guy could get caught in heavy weather and depend upon this contraption to get him out of it. It was really neat. It

An Interview with Jim Brown

almost seemed like magic when we finally got that thing to work on the Searunners.

Both cabins were sealable with hatches. They could be closed up tight in heavy weather. I was told by some of my clients who owned Searunner 25s that the central cockpit of these boats went through conditions that filled the cockpits to the brim with water. The boats were in waves where they were completely inundated with solid water in the cockpits, yet they just popped right back up and kept on going.

I've also been told this was true for those who sailed the 40-foot Searunners through heavy waves. This is why the cockpits were enabled with rapid self-bailing capability. The centerboard trunks were open in the cockpits so they could bail themselves out before the next wave, even if they were filled to the brim.

When I drew up plans for the Searunner 25, I'd already built up a clientele for larger boats. But the plans for this 25-footer really took off. We sold a lot of plans for it and lots of boats were built too. The thing is, those boats were all built in the period *before epoxy*. That means most of the Searunner 25s that got built up until around 1972 were built with exterior plywood and fiberglass sheathing with polyester resin. For the most part, they didn't last for decades.

It just so happens that I still have my Searunner 31. It's still around even though it's 37 years old and was built before epoxy started being used to build wooden boats. I sort of knew what I was doing when I built it though. And the fact I've been the only one to ever own it has also helped keep it preserved. My Searunner is still solid, ready to go anywhere. So while keeping a boat like mine in good shape is possible, it was beyond the skills most of the amateur boat builders had back then.

Most homebuilders in the pre-epoxy days of the late '60s just didn't understand how to build a more permanent multihull. James Wharram used to tell people that his cats would last for 10 years and many of them lasted a lot longer than that. But again, that was before epoxy came along. Wooden boats now can last for generations because of the use of epoxy.

Perhaps the zaniest thing I ever heard done with a Searunner 25 came from my friend Max Hemminger. Max built and sailed a very nice 25-footer in the mid 1960s. He was intent on the goal of single-hand sailing to Hawaii. So I helped him work out the wind-vane self-steering system in preparation for this trip.

When Max finally took off on his voyage it was rather late in the year … probably close to November. He was a purist and wanted to go without having an outboard motor on the boat. So he built hatches into the cockpit seats that could be removed in order to look down into the water from those hatch holes. Max installed oarlocks at those openings in order for him to stand in the cockpit and row the boat if he felt he needed to. He also fit turn-button hold-downs on those hatches.

When he took off on his voyage we were very concerned about him going to Hawaii so late in the year. So I set him up with a "tire drogue," a bridle used to slow a boat down during a storm, so it doesn't go too fast down the slope of one wave and then crash into another wave. We made Max's drogue using a tire and chain. (Whenever we went offshore we'd take a tire and chain in case we got into trouble. We'd refer to it as "*de-spair tire*").

Using winches inside the cockpit, the sailor could control the length of the drogue's bridle lines and use the tire to keep the boat under control in storm conditions. We put the tire used for this drogue in a special locker on the stern so it would be available if needed. All Max had to do was dump this thing into the water during a storm if necessary.

Well, sure enough, Max got out into the ocean and got caught in a North Pacific gale. The wind was blowing like crazy and the waves were huge. So Max decided to dump the tire drogue into the water. Apparently the tire was a little *too* effective. The boat started to be dragged backward through the breaking crest. The water was coming up underneath the wing and popped his oar hatches out. Water started flooding the cockpit. The bigger problem, however, was that his companion hatches were open at the time because he hadn't closed the drop boards. Water was pouring down into the main hull.

So there Max was, all by himself, out in the middle of a gale, with water pouring into the boat. So he decided to cast off the tire drogue. He just cut it loose and dumped it into the ocean. The moment he did that the boat immediately just *took off* … by itself … self-steering … half-full of water … while Max bailed. And the boat just kept on going, steering itself downwind, and half full of water.

Despite this mishap, Max did make it to Hawaii. I don't think he sailed the boat back though. I think he sold it over there and came back and built another boat.

"The Janganda, Now … the Seaclipper 20"

A friend of mine is a guy named Jo Hudson. He is a gifted artist and dedicated seafarer. Jo lives in Big Sur and I met him when I was there back in the early '60s. Jo has owned 9 of my designs through the years. The biggest one was a 45-footer. Four of these boats have been Windriders, one of my later designs. He owned two of the 16-foot Windriders and two of the 17-footers.

Jo decided 2 boats were necessary for a couple of reasons. He liked the idea of taking 2 smaller boats, which are single-handers, out sailing together because it's fun for 2 sailors to go out on separate boats with each other. It's almost like each sailor gets to "watch themselves" while sailing. So he and I made some rather extensive expeditions with the 16-footers in both Baja and in the area around San Francisco Bay near the Golden Gate. These trips included both simple day sails and extended camping trips.

We decided we'd like to do some more expedition type sailing in 2002 and that was when the Windrider 17 was introduced. We realized the 17 was big enough to put 2 guys on, including the camping gear and all the fresh water we'd require for about a week. We needed that kind of capacity because we were headed to the Sea of Cortez and that is a remote enough place where things can go wrong if you're not prepared.

We had both been there before and knew what we were doing. And we were also fortunate enough to find a couple more guys who wanted to go sailing with us. We needed 2 boats of sufficient size that would allow us to get all 4 guys onto the beach to bring in all of the gear. The 17-foot boat was simply too big for just 2 guys to drag up out of the surf when it was carrying everything.

So once we got the two 17-footers we made an expedition down to Baja and sailed in the Sea of Cortez. We had a great time. And having lived in Big Sur, both Jo and I always wanted to cruise that coast. But there is a stretch of coast that has 50 miles with no harbors. We knew we were going to have to shoot the surf and camp on beaches that were otherwise inaccessible because of the cliffs.

We started from Pebble Beach in Carmel and went down to the Big Sur coast and had an incredible experience. We also learned our lessons the hard way when it came to the surf down there. We were blessed with mild surf during our trip. But we still had some problems with it. We certainly learned a lot about trying to navigate through that kind of surf amid rocky beach areas. We also learned a lot about what is needed for such beach camping during our trip.

I figured that one thing we needed was a slightly larger boat that you could still drag up a beach, but one that a sailor could also spend the night on if they had to. In some of those places you really can't get ashore for the night. We encountered a couple of situations like that.

There are times when the surf will just be too big in places like the Sea of Cortez. Unless you're willing to shoot the waves you have to spend the night in a kelp bed. In other cases, the tide is so low that you'd have to drag the boat a quarter mile over rocks before getting to a beach where you could set up camp. So what we found ourselves really wanting during those times was a boat that we could drag almost any distance with impunity … but one that was also big enough for us to stay on board, overnight if necessary. The Windrider 17s were not quite big enough for us to be able to do that.

We decided we needed a boat that was just a little bigger too … one that offered enough distance between the crossbeams and enabled us to really stretch out. We needed about 7 to 8 feet between the crossbeams in order to use the side decks as a bunk platform. So with that in mind, I sat down and designed the boat I originally called the *Janganda*, which John Marples and I are now calling the *Seaclipper 20*.

Seaclipper 20 – sketch #1

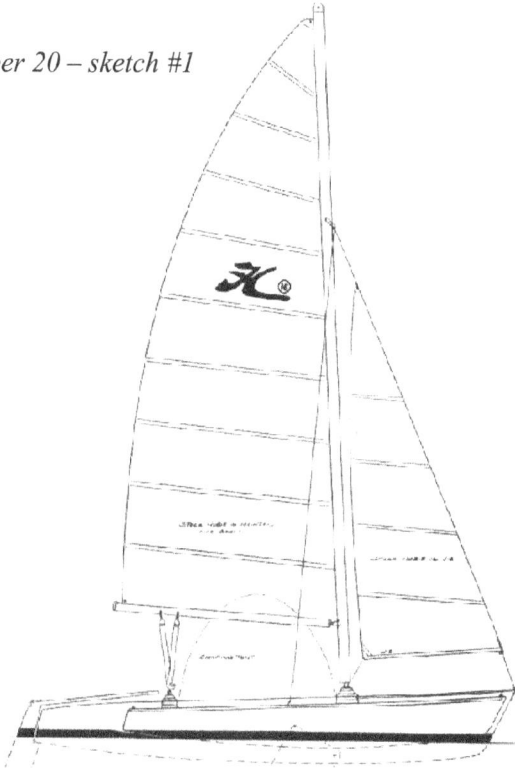

More Small Trimarans

I took the name Janganda from an ancient trimaran that is still in use on the east coast of Africa. I had a chance to see these boats during my travels and they were the most earthy, crude sailing vessels I'd ever seen. But they also had some features that tended to defy modern marine architects. They were just remarkable. They're also referred to as *Ungalawa*, depending upon what language is being spoken.

Seaclipper 20 – sketch #2

SEACLIPPER 20
JANGANDA
CAMPING CRUISER & DAYSAILER
SAIL & DECK PLAN
SCALE 3/8"=1'   REV: A DATE: 4/09

DESIGNED BY
JAMES W. BROWN
FOSTER, VA. 23056
COPYRIGHT © 2009 JAMES W. BROWN
DRAWN BY JOHN MARPLES

An Interview with Jim Brown

I designed my new boat to replicate the crudeness and simplicity of those boats, except in modern materials. I want a guy who has never been able to build anything more complex than a birdhouse to be able to put this thing together in his garage … perhaps with his son or daughter helping him.

The Seaclipper 20 is intended for sheet plywood construction. You can use very inexpensive materials for it and it'll turn out successfully.

I wanted it to be an "overnighter," but under the same conditions in which we'd camped on those Big Sur beaches. Sometimes we used a tent and sometimes we slept in the open, depending upon the conditions. So I wanted to be able to set up a tent on this boat that is big enough for 2 people. This suggested to me the need for a platform that is about 8 feet square, which can accommodate a standard 8-foot pop tent.

This tent platform will be 8 feet wide, but that is trailerable width without having to take anything apart. The crossbeams are designed to be "swing wing." The beams themselves will just be solid wooden planks. They'll swing out aft and then tuck back in underneath the platform when retracted. They'll be held in place with pins. The whole swing system on this boat will be very simple.

The platform I designed for the Seaclipper 20 has a footwell running down the middle of it that allows you to sit on the side decks and put your feet down into the footwell so you're not squatting on a trampoline when sailing. The side decks will be made of plywood because trampolines can get expensive and be rather problematic. They really don't last.

The footwell is deep enough that a sailor can sit on the side deck comfortably. So the footwell is the cockpit of this boat. The centerboard operates below the cockpit sole. So when you're camping onboard you won't have a big daggerboard sticking up in the middle of the tent. It's a swing centerboard that lives entirely below the cockpit sole.

The tent used by campers on this boat would have to be modified a little bit. The bottom would have to be cut out to some extent so that you could sit with your feet in the footwell if you wanted. But the tent would protect the adventurers from rain and bugs and wind. You could even pull out your galley box and fix yourself a meal while staying right on board the boat if the circumstances suggested that it wouldn't be wise to try and beach the boat for the night. The great thing about this boat is that the platform is always in place so that campers will be able to spend the night on it whether they're on a beach or out in the anchorage.

This boat features a flat bottom on the main hull. And while it does work against performance under sail, it works great for being able to drag the boat up a beach on rollers. (We found a source for lightweight air rollers as the result of our experience camp-cruising at Big Sur).

The boat will be built using fiberglass sheathing and epoxy. And then, if you want to be able to drag it up rocky beaches without damaging it, you'll sheath the flat hull bottom with a layer of quarter inch thick U.H.M.W. (Ultra High Molecular Weight) Polyethylene. This is the stuff used on places like ferry docks, so boats can scuff up against this material on the landing without getting damaged. This stuff is "scuff proof." Applying it to the bottom of this boat would allow it to be dragged down a highway for miles without suffering damage. It's just incredible material.

As far as a mast goes, this boat is intended to receive any beach cat rig. There are a lot of them around. The most expensive part of building a boat is often the sails and rigging and hardware. This boat is intended to take advantage of the surplus of beach cats whose hulls have been torn up racing, while the mast and sails are still available and in reasonably good condition.

This boat would respond well to rigs like the Hobie 16 or 18 or 21. There are also lots of other beach cats in this size range too.

The floats will be very simple to build. They may end up being a little canted on the final design.

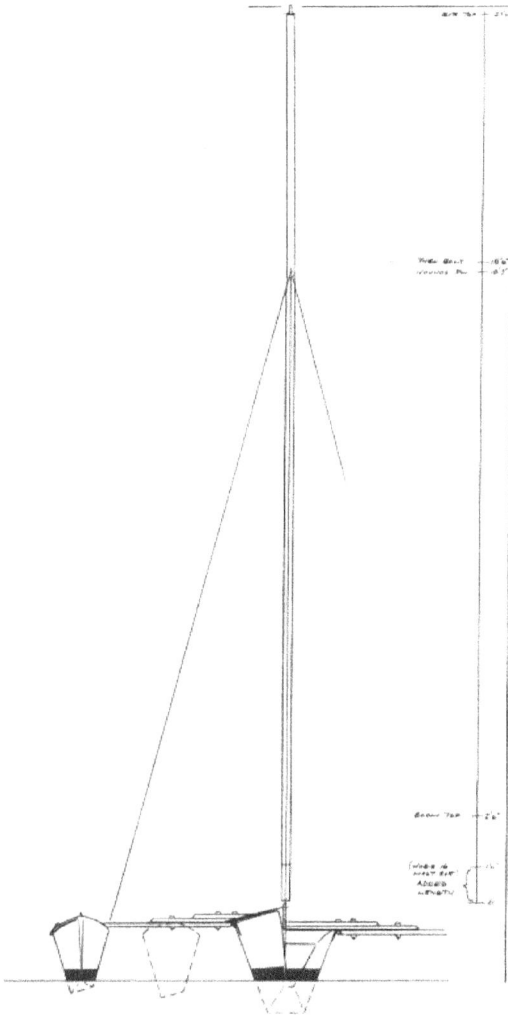

Seaclipper 20 – sketch #3

One thing that would be great to have with this boat would be block and tackle material or a winch of some type. I'm aware of a chainsaw type of tool that replaced the saw blade with a winch.

More Small Trimarans

It was used to drag logs out of the woods. If you had one of those things on board with you then the boat is the perfect size to be moved by that kind of thing. If you used one of those you could practically drag this boat up a cliff.

We learned from Windriders that you can get great performance out of trimarans this size without having to overpower them. A trimaran doesn't have to be overpowered in order to be fast. So the sailing performance of this boat may be surprising, despite it's rugged simplicity.

"Smaller Trailerable Multihulls"

In my opinion, having a small trailerable multihull is the way to go today for many sailors. The economy has taken quite a toll on the marine industry, particularly when it comes to bigger boats.

Most trimarans in the '60s were built very inexpensively. I'm very dismayed that multihull sailing has almost "high-teched" itself into obscurity because of high costs. When I built my first Piver Frolic, it cost me $200 – plus sails. Piver's original boat cost $200 *with* sails. He had made his own sails with Mylar film stuck together with scotch tape. They rattled like crazy in the wind. But as far as I knew the sails were just Mylar drafting film.

Then my 24-foot Nugget – the boat my wife and I took out to sea – was launched for about $2,000. Some of the early Searunner 25s were built for about $3,000 during the 1960s, using all lumberyard materials, plus fiberglass sheathing. What's happened now is that there is a tremendous gap between something like the Windrider 16, which is a popular small trimaran, and something like the smaller Farriers, which cost tens of thousands of dollars to build.

I think the multihull community has really lost out here because we haven't purposely trained many younger sailors on how to inexpensively acquire their own boats. Most multis are just too expensive.

An Interview with Jim Brown

Meade Gougeon and I just got back from a month-long trip. We traveled down the western coast of the US and stopped by every boat yard, walked inside every marine store, and spoke to every boat builder we could. We discovered that some owners are simply abandoning their large boats. Some of them are struggling with paying the notes on both their home and their big boat.

A few desperate boat owners are even taking large boats out into the water and sinking them. Nevertheless, it was the biggest year ever for the Port Townsend Wooden Boat Festival/show (2009). If I'm right, this suggests there is going to be a lot of demand for smaller, trailerable boats. We really got a sense at the boat show that people were looking for boats they can get onto a trailer in order to avoid paying the fees that go with mooring and storing large watercraft.

The harbors are being clogged by abandoned large boats, harbormasters are having trouble collecting the rent on them, dry storage yards are jammed (and expensive) and even launching large boats can be quite an undertaking these days. What is required during times like this are boats that don't even require a launching ramp. This makes smaller, trailerable multihulls ideal. I think they've turned out to be THE way for most sailors to be able to go out onto the water nowadays.

"A Multihull History Project"

I'm currently opening up a fascinating multihull history project website. It's been challenging because there isn't a whole lot of archeological evidence about ancient multihulls because those boats were all constructed of 100% vegetable fiber. There is just nothing left of those ancient vessels.

By the time Europeans arrived in the Pacific during the 1600s, the island cultures of Polynesia and Micronesia had been in decline for up to 400 years. The classic Polynesian period ended about 1200 A.D. This means we're not certain just how far back multihull vessels go.

The fact is, though, that single and double outrigger canoes spread all the way across the Pacific and into the Indian Ocean to East Africa. This means those who sailed multihulls had a wide distribution throughout the world.

I think the trimaran may have been the first multihull – by way of the double outrigger canoe. The preponderance of evidence suggests the ancient peoples in what is now Viet Nam used trimarans to successfully move out to the Philippines.

I had the opportunity to work on a boat-building training program in the Philippines in the early '80s. When I was there, the official government estimate of the number of their *Banca* trimarans was 700,000. It turns out that their vessels of choice are still these double outrigger canoes.

The Banca trimaran is like a car for many people in the Philippines. They attach motors to them now for traveling all over. Some American soldiers stationed over there started putting the engines used to pump out trenches onto these boats. And it caught on with the locals. They're often referred to in English now as "Pump Boats."

The racing version of these double outrigger canoes is the *Paraw*. They have a huge native regatta with these racing boats each year. It's a real celebration of sail.

A big part of my history project has been collecting multihull stories from a variety of sources. I've worked with a fellow named Scott Brown (no relation), who is a Canadian cinematographer. We've collected interviews from many modern multihull trailblazers of the 20th century. Those interviews are in video format right now.

I've also collected other stories related to multihull history from all over. They include the background and lore of multihulls from the ancient past to the present. These stories will probably be offered in both print and audio book download versions very soon. I hope to include a bit of the storytelling myself in the audios.

An Interview with Jim Brown

I've also written many stories and collected them inside 2 books, which will soon be self-published. The first book will be my memoir of the early days of multihull development up until about 1975. The 2nd book relates to the 2nd half of my career, which covers my efforts around the world to develop multihull workboats. I share a lot about my work on those boat-building projects overseas during the 1980s. I've got lots of stories from those years that I'd love to publish. Some folks really seem to enjoy them.

....

For more about the Seaclipper 20 Trimaran, and the other designs of Jim Brown and his partner John Marples, see
http://www.searunner.com
For more stories of multihull history, see Jim Brown's website
http://www.outrig.org

295

www.ingramcontent.com/pod-product-compliance
Lightning Source LLC
Chambersburg PA
CBHW050109280326
41933CB00010B/1028